T0357719

LOVE &
NUMBERS

LOVE &
NUMBERS

USING NUMEROLOGY
TO DECODE YOUR
RELATIONSHIPS

——— • • • ———

HANS DECOZ

A TarcherPerigee Book

tarcherperigee

an imprint of Penguin Random House LLC
1745 Broadway, New York, NY 10019
penguinrandomhouse.com

Copyright © 2025 Hans Decoz
Penguin Random House values and supports copyright. Copyright fuels creativity,
encourages diverse voices, promotes free speech, and creates a vibrant culture.
Thank you for buying an authorized edition of this book and for complying with
copyright laws by not reproducing, scanning, or distributing any part of it in
any form without permission. You are supporting writers and allowing
Penguin Random House to continue to publish books for every reader.
TarcherPerigee with tp colophon is a registered trademark of Penguin Random
House LLC. Please note that no part of this book may be used or reproduced in any
manner for the purpose of training artificial intelligence technologies or systems.

Most TarcherPerigee books are available at special quantity discounts for bulk
purchase for sales promotions, premiums, fundraising, and educational needs.
Special books or book excerpts also can be created to fit specific needs. For details,
write: SpecialMarkets@penguinrandomhouse.com.

Library of Congress Cataloging-in-Publication Data has been applied for.
Trade paperback ISBN: 9780593330555
eBook ISBN: 9780593330562

Printed in the United States of America
1st Printing

The authorized representative in the EU for product safety and compliance
is Penguin Random House Ireland, Morrison Chambers, 32 Nassau Street,
Dublin D02 YH68, Ireland, https://eu-contact.penguin.ie.

Book design by Daniel Brount

Contents

— • • • —

CONTENTS

PART 3: THE IMPORTANCE OF YOUR CYCLES

This book is dedicated to Willy van Eck.

LOVE &
NUMBERS

PART 1

Of Love and Romance

CHAPTER 1

The Love We Seek

Do you remember the first time you fell in love? One moment, hope and joy fill your heart to bursting, and the next, angst and anxiety threaten to push you over the edge. We have all been there because it is essential to being human. We need love like we need air.

As far back as the beginning of recorded history, human beings have written stories and sung songs about love. We have gone to war for the sake of love, built palaces to honor our love, and traveled the earth in search of love.

And yet, no one has ever seen love. Think about that for a minute. We see reflections of love everywhere. We feel love, and its presence is undeniable. We see love in the faces of parents and their children, of young lovers and of old lovers. We see the effect of love, and its beauty can make us cry tears of joy, but we don't actually *see* love. Like gravity, only the influence it has on everything it touches can be seen, but you don't see the stuff itself. Love is invisible, and yet, it is the most powerful force we can experience. It binds people for life. It has been said that love is the reason we exist, that love is the reason everything exists.

Love is the gravity of the unseen world. We orbit one another, and it is love that binds us. From the day you are born, you are in a universe of love in which you orbit your parents, and your parents orbit you, where your brothers and sisters and uncles and aunts and teachers and so many others circle you and one another in a multidimensional universe, performing an endless dance of love. We are all connected, forward and backward in time, and in all directions, we share the same space and the same power; this is the magic of love.

Love is invisible, yet more real than the world of matter. Love, like gravity, affects you, me, all of us, and all living creatures without ever revealing itself, without showing what it is made of; it is a powerful, invisible force that, for reasons no one can claim to truly understand, appears to be the source and the purpose of our existence.

Love. No wonder we can't stop singing and writing and dancing about it. And I promise you, if we ever encounter aliens from a galaxy far, far away, love will be the reason they exist, and the gift of love will be no less powerful and important to them than it is for us.

And then there is romance, love with a twist, love designed for procreation, love that can thrill us or torture us, and sometimes both at the same time. When we are young, we are extremely vulnerable, and you might say that a broken heart is a rite of passage. When you are older, a broken heart may hurt no less than when you were young, but experience has taught us that this too will pass.

When you are in love, you are prepared to do anything to make it last, and that means recognizing where you differ and how to maintain harmony. It often also means you have to work on yourself to become a better person, to make your partner happy. In this way, a romantic relationship can also be a cause of self-improvement, and that is always a good thing.

Numerology can help you understand your own personality as well as your partner's to a degree that you can prevent unnecessary friction and avoid the pitfalls that can cause a relationship to fail. In this book, you will learn to read your own numbers, and the numbers of your loved one, in order to dive deeper into your relationship with them and ultimately make it stronger.

Relationships and the benefits of numerology

Numerology has been around for thousands of years. Every culture in the world has developed some form of numerology, including the Chinese, Japanese, Greeks, Hebrews, Egyptians, Phoenicians, early Christians, Mayans, and Incas, all of whom utilized numerology to gain a deeper understanding of themselves and the universe. Pythagorean numerology is the most popular system of numerology in the Western world, and it is the method used in this book. It is thought to have been established by the Greek philosopher and mathematician Pythagoras, who is believed to have integrated the mathematical disciplines of Arabic, Druid, Phoenician, Egyptian, and Essene sciences.

Over time, Pythagorean numerology has continued to evolve, forming the spiritual foundation for many secret societies, such as the Rosicrucians, Freemasons, and Anthroposophists.

Numerology's popularity has increased dramatically over the past five or six decades, and frequently appears as a plot device in fiction. Sometimes it serves as a casual, comedic element, as in the 1950s TV sitcom *I Love Lucy* episode titled "The Séance," where Lucy experiments with numerology. Other times, numerology is central to the storyline. For instance, the movie π features a protagonist who encounters a numerologist searching for hidden numerical patterns in the Torah. The TV show *Touch* centers almost entirely on numerology's role in the events and coincidences of people's lives. Similarly, the movie *The Number 23*, starring Jim Carrey, revolves around the purported mysteries of the number 23, which Discordianists believed to be a holy number.

Some famous people and celebrities have shown an interest in or belief in numerology. Sir Isaac Newton, the renowned mathematician and physicist, is said to have had an interest in numerology and alchemy, exploring the mystical aspects of numbers alongside his scientific work.

Carl Jung, the influential psychologist and psychoanalyst, was known to have an interest in numerology, particularly in relation to his theories on archetypes and the collective unconscious. Some more current celebrities who have shown an interest in numerology are Nicolas Cage, Madonna, David Beckham (known to have a preference for the number 7, which has significance in numerology and has been his jersey number for many years), Lady Gaga, and Khloé Kardashian, to name a few.

At its root, numerology is an attempt to recognize patterns. It uses your birth data to extract a range of numbers that can be interpreted to help you understand more about who you are, your personality traits, your likes and dislikes, talents, weaknesses, and more.

The desire to impress the people we love is deeply rooted in our core nature. All living creatures have mating rituals designed to attract their intended partners. As humans, we possess the unique ability to transcend this basic desire, striving for deep and enduring intimacy.

Understanding the nuances of your partner can significantly contribute to sustaining happy, long-term relationships. By recognizing and appreciating these subtleties, you can foster a more meaningful and fulfilling connection. Additionally, gaining insights into someone you've just started dating can only enhance your chances of building a strong foundation for a future relationship. Whether the relationship is new or well established, knowing more about the other person is always beneficial.

Numerology is by no means perfect—it is an inexact science, and for that reason you should apply your own analytical powers and common sense. Think of it as a weather report; it can be close, but it's not always right. However, people have fine-tuned this art for thousands of years.

We have recognized the patterns, the links between numbers found in your chart and the characteristics that make you uniquely you. Use it like a tool; it will not shape or change anything—that's your job. But it can inspire you to change yourself, and that is priceless. Your personal evolutionary growth is the deciding factor in your happiness, and this means you are in charge—perhaps not of everything that comes your way, but you are always in control of your response. This is a truth we should all be conscious of.

The key to a long and loving relationship

Numerology's main indicator of who you are, and who you will become over time, is your Life Path number. It reveals the main character traits and needs that define the relationship between you and your romantic partner. Your Life Path number shows the main causes of the initial attraction, as well as what is needed to maintain and grow the relationship into a stable and fulfilling one. When you know and understand your own Life Path and that of your partner, you are better able to make the love of your life a lasting and happy one. The power and influence of your Life Path number cannot be overstated.

When you are in a relationship, you come to know each other more deeply over time. At first, friction is rare, but as time goes by and you discover additional sides to your partner, you become aware of personality traits you appreciate, as well as some that rub you the wrong way. Even if you consider your relationship nearly perfect, you will experience occasional bouts of conflict.

Negative traits are almost always a cause of friction, but it is interesting to note that some qualities that are considered positive can also be incompatible. My approach is designed to throw light on differences in your personalities that might benefit from a frank, unbiased examination. For example, if a person has a 5 Life Path and their partner has a 4, they possess directly opposite personality traits. A 5 Life Path individual is unconventional, spontaneous, dynamic, impulsive, and generally unorganized. They thrive on chaos, love change, think on their feet, and are highly adaptable. Conversely, a 4 Life Path person prefers predictability, stability, and routine. They are organized, detail oriented, dislike change, and abhor chaos.

When these two first meet, it may seem unlikely that they would be attracted to each other. However, if they invest the time and effort to understand each other, their relationship can become fulfilling and enduring. They complement each other and provide what the other needs—the 4 offers a stabilizing presence for the 5, while the 5 brings excitement and adventure to the 4. This harmony is achievable only if they understand each other's needs and desires and respect and tolerate their differences.

CHAPTER 2

The Life Path

Some aspects of numerology can involve double-digit numbers that are significant in your personal life. However, when it comes to relationship compatibility, only the nine fundamental Life Path numbers (1 through 9) are essential, and that is what this book will focus on.

Finding your Life Path number

Life Path numbers are easy to calculate. All you need to do is reduce your date of birth to a single digit—it's a few simple steps that require nothing more than adding one single-digit number to another. However, if you don't like math, even simple math, feel free to skip ahead to page 12 to find your Life Path number without the effort.

Calculate your Life Path number the easy way

Step 1.

Take your month of birth and, if needed, reduce it to a single digit. For example, May is 5 and requires no math, but December is the 12th month, which means we have to add 1 + 2. The result is 3. The month of December therefore reduces to 3. November, the 11th month, reduces to a single digit by adding 1 + 1, for a 2. And October reduces to one digit by adding 1 + 0 = 1.

Step 2.

Take your day of birth and, if needed, reduce it to a single digit. For example, if you were born on the 15th day of the month, reduce 15 by adding 1 + 5, for a 6.

Step 3.

Do the same with your year of birth. For example, someone born in 1994 would reduce 1994 by adding 1 + 9 + 9 + 4, which equals 23. Then further reduce 23 by adding 2 + 3, for a 5.

Step 4.

Add the three results and reduce to a single digit.

In our example, we found the month of December to be a 3, the day to be a 6, and the year to be a 5. Add 3 + 6 + 5 = 14. Then reduce 14 by adding 1 + 4 = 5.

That's it. The Life Path number is 5.

In another example, someone born August 5, 2001, would add 8 (for August) + 5 (the day of birth) + 3 (the year of birth 2001 reduces to 3 after adding 2 + 0 + 0 + 1). This person's Life Path is 8 + 5 + 3 = 16, which then reduces to 7 by adding 1 + 6.

Go ahead and calculate your own Life Path number. Or simply use the tables below to find it.

Make a note of the number where your calendar day of birth and month of birth intersect in the chart on the following page. This is called your Sun Number and is used to find other cycles.

Sun Number

MONTH OF BIRTH

DAY OF BIRTH	January and October	February and November	March and December	April	May	June	July	August	September
1, 10, 19, 28	2	3	4	5	6	7	8	9	1
2, 11, 20, 29	3	4	5	6	7	8	9	1	2
3, 12, 21, 30	4	5	6	7	8	9	1	2	3
4, 13, 22, 31	5	6	7	8	9	1	2	3	4
5, 14, 23	6	7	8	9	1	2	3	4	5
6, 15, 24	7	8	9	1	2	3	4	5	6
7, 16, 25	8	9	1	2	3	4	5	6	7
8. 17, 26	9	1	2	3	4	5	6	7	8
9, 18, 27	1	2	3	4	5	6	7	8	9

Your Life Path number is found on the intersection of your calendar year of birth and your Sun Number in the chart below.

Life Path

	SUN NUMBER								
YEAR OF BIRTH	**1**	**2**	**3**	**4**	**5**	**6**	**7**	**8**	**9**
1930, 1939, 1948, 1957, 1966, 1975, 1984, 1993, 2002, 2011, 2020, 2029	5	6	7	8	9	1	2	3	4
1931, 1940, 1949, 1958, 1967, 1976, 1985, 1994, 2003, 2012, 2021, 2030	6	7	8	9	1	2	3	4	5
1932, 1941, 1950, 1959, 1968, 1977, 1986, 1995, 2004, 2013, 2022, 2031	7	8	9	1	2	3	4	5	6
1933, 1942, 1951, 1960, 1969, 1978, 1987, 1996, 2005, 2014, 2023, 2032	8	9	1	2	3	4	5	6	7
1934, 1943, 1952, 1961, 1970, 1979, 1988, 1997, 2006, 2015, 2024, 2033	9	1	2	3	4	5	6	7	8
1935, 1944, 1953, 1962, 1971, 1980, 1989, 1998, 2007, 2016, 2025, 2034	1	2	3	4	5	6	7	8	9
1936, 1945, 1954, 1963, 1972, 1981, 1990, 1999, 2008, 2017, 2026, 2035	2	3	4	5	6	7	8	9	1
1937, 1946, 1955, 1964, 1973, 1982, 1991, 2000, 2009, 2018, 2027, 2036	3	4	5	6	7	8	9	1	2
1938, 1947, 1956, 1965, 1974, 1983, 1992, 2001, 2010, 2019, 2028, 2037	4	5	6	7	8	9	1	2	3

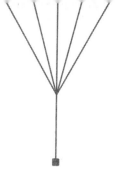

Life Path Numbers and Their Meaning

If there was ever a pivotal moment, it was the moment of your birth. In that instant, you entered a new reality—the reality of human life and human consciousness. But even at that moment, you were a person with your own unique character, as unique as your DNA.

Your first breath marked the beginning of your journey on the road we call your Life Path. Your Life Path number gives a broad outline of the opportunities, challenges, and lessons you encounter throughout your life. It also reveals the strengths, specific talents, and characteristics you were given to help you overcome challenges and evolve into the best you can be.

1 Life Path

A Life Path 1 is a primal force, a natural-born leader. You have an unwavering belief in your right to make your own decisions, insisting on freedom of thought and action. With your drive and determination, you refuse to let anything or anyone hinder your path once you're committed to a goal. You willingly shoulder the responsibility of protecting and providing for your loved ones.

You are a commanding presence and demand respect and attention. When things don't go your way, you can become irritated and domineering. You prefer to be at the forefront, seeking the limelight. Your creativity and originality set you apart, and you're unafraid to deviate from conventional paths to solve problems. Impatience with your own and others' shortcomings can be a challenge.

Status and the appearance of success matter to you. You strive for growth, success, and the finer things in life. Beware of selfishness, conceit, and excessive concern with appearances. Keep an eye on overzealous behavior, anger, and aggressiveness, as they could lead to domineering, vindictive, or violent tendencies.

In the business and career realm, you excel when left to your own devices. Owning your own business and being your own boss is ideal for you. Pursue your life's dream with unwavering determination while managing stress, maintaining a healthy diet, and enjoying a suitable exercise routine. Competitive sports, particularly those involving running and swimming, can be a healthy outlet for your drive.

Remember that your talents and abilities are gifts from a higher source, promoting gratitude and humility rather than pride and conceit. A Life Path 1 often achieves great success in life when they fully employ their drive, creativity, originality, and pioneering spirit.

2 Life Path

If your Life Path is 2, you embody the essence of a Peacemaker and possess the soul of an artist. Your character is defined by your exceptional sensitivity, perceptiveness, and a touch of shyness. These qualities serve as both your strengths and weaknesses. Your heightened sensitivity enables you to connect deeply with your own emotions and those of others, yet it may also lead you to hold back and suppress your considerable talents.

Your innate sensitivity and perceptiveness grant you a profound understanding of people's wants and feelings, making you an expert in diplomacy and tact. Patience and cooperation are second nature to you, allowing you to excel in group settings and harmonize diverse opinions.

You find solace in music and poetry, thriving in harmonious environments. Your keen eye for beauty, coupled with a remarkable sense of balance and rhythm, adds an artistic flair to your life. You possess healing abilities, particularly in fields like massage, acupuncture, physical therapy, and counseling. However, your sensitivity can sometimes be your Achilles' heel.

Your ego is fragile, easily wounded by thoughtless remarks or criticisms from others. Consequently, you might withhold your own thoughts and contributions to avoid conflict, leading to simmering resentment and anger. Confrontation is often avoided as you seek to escape battles.

Yet, within you lies significant inner strength waiting to be tapped. When you embrace this strength, you unlock the power to navigate challenging situations toward your goals, drawing upon your heightened awareness and diplomatic skills. Your profound perceptiveness extends to your role as a lover, enabling you to cater to your partner's needs and desires with a nearly magical finesse. However, if you feel mistreated or jilted, you can respond with formidable force, occasionally resorting to personal criticisms vindictively.

Your diplomatic prowess, organizational talents, and awareness enable you to accomplish demanding tasks effectively. You often choose to work behind the scenes, facilitating the success of your endeavors without seeking the limelight. Unfortunately, your contributions may not always receive the recognition they deserve, leading to underestimation and overlooked accomplishments. Rather than brooding over these losses, it's essential to confront those who undervalue your contributions and stand up for your achievements.

Security, comfort, tranquil settings, and the company of loved ones are crucial to your well-being. You possess a perfectionist streak, evident in your tasteful and well-maintained home and work environments. As a companion, you are a delightful presence with a keen sense of humor. Friends seek your calming and peaceful company, viewing you as a safe haven for other sensitive souls who appreciate your compassion and understanding.

Once you discover your niche in life, all your talents and intelligence can lead to significant success. Seek out work that allows your sensitive nature to flourish, helping you become the glue that binds others together.

3 Life Path

Individuals with a Life Path of 3 are endowed with an exceptional talent for creativity and self-expression. Many renowned writers, poets, actors, and musicians find themselves under the influence of the 3 Life Path. You possess a quick wit, a natural gift for conversation, and an innate attraction to the spotlight.

Your reservoir of artistic abilities is so abundant that you may have been drawn to the arts from a very young age. However, harnessing your artistic potential requires unwavering discipline and a wholehearted commitment to its genuine development.

Dedication, unwavering focus, and relentless hard work are the indispensable tools needed to unlock your talents fully. Your gift for self-expression places you at the center of attention, making you the life of any gathering. Yet, there's a risk of squandering your talents if you allow yourself to become too socially oriented, flitting like a social butterfly.

Your creativity is a precious gift that can grant you the comfort and luxury you desire, but only with persistent concentration and discipline. You possess a natural optimism and the resilience to overcome numerous setbacks. Your sociable nature renders you popular, and your sunny, happy-go-lucky attitude inspires those around you. You're often generous to a fault.

However, it's common for many individuals born under the 3 Life Path to grapple with financial management due to disorganization and a lack of seriousness when it comes to responsibilities. Emotionally, you are sensitive and vulnerable. When hurt, you retreat behind a veil of silence, eventually emerging with jokes and laughter that mask your true emotions. In times of depression, you can become moody and cynical, sometimes resorting to sarcastic remarks that may inadvertently hurt those in your vicinity.

When channeled positively, your talent for self-expression becomes a formidable force of inspiration in the world, uplifting others and leading to substantial success and happiness for yourself.

4 Life Path

Having a 4 Life Path signifies that you possess a practical, down-to-earth nature and a firm sense of right and wrong. You are often referred to as the "Salt of the Earth." Your character is marked by orderliness, organization, systematic thinking, and self-control. You approach problem-solving with a methodical, step-by-step, and rational methodology. Once you commit to a course of action, you display unwavering determination and don't easily give up.

You are not one to be swayed by "get rich quick" schemes. Instead, you believe in the value of hard work and long hours to build a solid foundation in your business or career. Precision, tenacity, and perseverance are your hallmarks, and you have immense potential for success, but it often requires considerable effort to overcome the challenges and limitations that frequently come your way. Justice and honesty hold a sacred place in your heart, making you a dependable and trustworthy cornerstone in your community.

While you may not naturally lean toward idealism (as the 4 is a realist), you are willing to work toward a better world in a practical and realistic manner. However, you should be cautious about being inflexible in your ideas and too quick to judge others. Your loyalty to those you love is unwavering, and you excel in collaborative efforts.

When you are part of a team, it's crucial that you have a well-defined responsibility that doesn't overlap with those of others, as this is when you perform at your best. You must guard against being bossy and rude, recognizing that not everyone can match your rare levels of discipline and perseverance.

You handle money with care and appreciate the security of a financial cushion. Your strong work ethic often leads you to start your career early in life. However, your methodical nature can sometimes make you rigid and resistant to change, causing you to miss valuable opportunities.

Cultivating flexibility in your character is essential. While you are well suited for marriage and often become a responsible and loving parent, anything that disrupts your profound sense of order, such as separation or divorce, can be profoundly unsettling. In such situations, you may become obsessed and even seek your own version of justice, sometimes with a sense of vengeance.

You possess courage and are a true survivor. Your hard work and adherence to traditional values pay off, providing you with the rewards you seek and rightfully deserve.

5 Life Path

Having a 5 Life Path defines you as a Dynamic Force, and the core of your personality is freedom. You thrive on the thrill of travel, adventure, variety, and meeting new people. Your curiosity knows no bounds, and you have an insatiable desire to experience all that life has to offer. You enjoy juggling multiple activities, as long as you're not tied down to any single pursuit.

Change, novelty, and expanding horizons are your lifeblood. You possess a natural ability to form friendships effortlessly, and your up-beat personality often inspires and attracts people from diverse back-grounds.

Words flow easily for you, and you possess a remarkable talent for motivating others. Careers in sales, advertising, publicity, promotion, politics, or any field that requires strong communication skills and a deep understanding of people are well suited to you. However, discipline and order may not come naturally, and you can occasionally act on im-pulse, leading to decisions or expressions you later regret.

The pursuit of freedom and adventure sometimes leads those born with a 5 Life Path to struggle with issues like substance abuse, overin-dulgence in food or pleasure, or simply not making the most of life's opportunities.

You are sensual by nature and relish savoring all of life's pleasures. Sensual experiences, including those related to food, sex, and other sen-sory delights, are integral to your enjoyment of life.

In matters of relationships, you find it challenging to commit to just one person, but when you do, your loyalty can be unwavering, akin to that of a faithful old dog.

Your diverse talents encompass a wide range of abilities, but to truly succeed, you must harness discipline and unwavering focus, which are the keys to unlocking your full potential. Without these, many of your ventures may remain unfinished, and you might not fully realize the ex-tent of your abilities. Nevertheless, with hard work and perseverance, your potential knows no bounds.

During your younger years, you may have been perceived as a wild child by adults, causing concern within your family. Don't rush your choice of career; you often mature later in life and require a broad range of experiences before discovering and wholeheartedly committing to your true calling.

For individuals with a 5 Life Path, the ultimate challenge is to grasp the genuine meaning of freedom. Your world is marked by constant change, demanding adaptability, and courage. It's vital to maintain a regular exercise routine to keep your body in good shape and maintain flexibility, promoting inner security and confidence.

Your longing for freedom often draws you toward self-employment. Your task is to settle into one area and cultivate your abilities sufficiently to earn a living and achieve success.

Once you've found your niche as a 5 Life Path, the motivation and inspiration you offer others will lead to reciprocal support and promotion from friends and colleagues on your path to success.

6 Life Path

A Life Path 6 individual embodies remarkable compassion and possesses a strong desire to be of service to others. You are the quintessential Caretaker, always looking out for the well-being of those around you. You hold a deep concern for the weak and downtrodden, naturally gravitating toward the roles of healer and helper. Offering comfort to those in need comes naturally to you, and you readily provide a shoulder for others to lean on.

Your life's mission is to develop the tools required to offer genuine and effective assistance to others, transcending the role of a sympathetic listener. Striking the delicate balance between help and interference is key for you.

Much like a counselor, you must learn when to step back and allow others to navigate their struggles independently, preserving the essential experiences and lessons of life. Your inherent sense of balance equips you to support and stabilize others during challenging times.

As a 6 Life Path, you find it natural to assume responsibility, often filling the void left by others, and you don't shy away from personal sacrifice. There may be moments when you feel burdened by the trials of those around you, but the love and gratitude bestowed upon you by others are well-deserved rewards. Despite the admiration and adoration you receive, you remain humble, though you carry a deep sense of pride. You excel at maintaining harmony within your family or social group, adeptly reconciling and harmonizing divergent energies.

Maintaining physical health and fitness may require some effort, so it's essential to incorporate regular exercise into your routine while keeping your indulgence in sweets and dairy in check to prevent unwanted weight gain.

Marriage is something you actively seek, and you often prove to be a wonderful parent, offering warmth, protection, and understanding to your children. Your generosity, kindness, and physical attractiveness draw people to you.

In your youth, it's crucial to avoid choosing partners for the wrong reasons. Guard against allowing sentimentality to cloud your judgment, particularly when making decisions about a life partner. Your innate desire to be needed can sometimes lead you into relationships that aren't truly fulfilling or nurturing. It's important to discern between those you can genuinely help and those who may become weaker due to your care. Your natural inclination is to assist those who are less fortunate, but balance is key.

Your most significant temptation and potential pitfall lies in the belief that you must shoulder the world's burdens and save everyone. You possess an innate musical talent, as well as considerable aptitude in the visual and performing arts. However, your creativity may be stifled due to your willingness to sacrifice for others or your failure to fully recognize your talents. This is not to say you cannot excel in artistic pursuits; on the contrary, with dedication, you can find success in various artistic fields.

Additionally, you possess remarkable business acumen. With a 6 Life Path, you are graced with a considerable amount of charm and charisma, which you use effectively to attract the people and support you need to thrive in your endeavors.

7 Life Path

A 7 Life Path is an ardent inquirer and a truth enthusiast. You embody the role of the Seeker, possessing a profound and unwavering sense of yourself as a spiritual being. Consequently, your life's journey revolves around exploring the uncharted territories and unraveling the mysteries of existence.

You are admirably equipped for this mission. Armed with a brilliant mind, you are a highly analytical thinker, capable of deep concentration and theoretical insights. Research and assembling the pieces of intellectual puzzles deeply engage you. Once you've gathered enough fragments, your capacity for ingenious insights and practical problem-solving shines.

The 7 Life Path cherishes solitude and often thrives when working independently. You require uninterrupted periods to contemplate your ideas without the interference of external thoughts. You are a lone wolf, living by your own rules and methods. Consequently, forming and sustaining close relationships, particularly marriage, can be challenging for you. Your need for personal space and privacy is paramount, and any infringement on them can lead to frustration and irritation.

However, when your life is in equilibrium, you exhibit both charm and attractiveness. You can become the life of the party, relishing the opportunity to perform before an audience. Your wit and knowledge captivate others, especially the opposite sex. Nonetheless, you do have well-defined boundaries.

While you are generous in social settings, readily sharing your attention and energy, you keenly sense the necessity to "step off the stage" and return to the solace of your inner world. You associate peace with the unobtrusive privacy of your personal domain, making intimacy a complex terrain for you. You guard your inner world with fierce determination, much like a mother lion protects her cubs.

Yet, this penchant for privacy and solitude can lead to isolation and loneliness if taken to the extreme. As a 7 Life Path, you may experience an inner void, a yearning for companionship that remains unfulfilled.

Isolation at its extreme may give rise to cynicism and suspicion. Hidden, self-serving motives might develop, perceptible to others and causing discomfort in their presence. It is vital to guard against excessive withdrawal and self-reliance, which can obstruct the flow of love from others and deny you the genuine joy of friendship and close companionship. Watch out for selfishness and self-centeredness, as these may lead you to perceive yourself as the universe's center, diminishing the significance of others. Social interactions offer your perspective on life and yourself, while excessive isolation can narrow your worldview and disconnect you from the rest of humanity.

Inwardly, you may harbor feelings of envy toward those who easily form relationships. You might perceive others as more uninhibited or expressive than yourself, and you may harshly criticize your perceived lack of sociability, authority, or leadership skills.

Your life's challenge is to uphold your independence without succumbing to feelings of isolation or ineffectiveness. It's crucial to retain your unique perspective while remaining open to the insights and knowledge others offer. With your innate ability to learn, analyze, and explore life's profound questions, you possess immense potential for personal growth and success. As you approach middle age, you will exude refinement and wisdom, a testament to your lifelong journey.

Pythagoras held the number seven in high regard due to its immense spiritual potential. You are inherently gifted with natural leadership abilities and the capacity to amass substantial wealth. Your talent for effective management extends to all aspects of life, particularly in business and financial matters. You possess an innate understanding of the material world, intuitively grasping the inner workings of virtually any endeavor.

You have the remarkable power to inspire people to join you in your pursuits, although they may struggle to see what you see. Consequently, those around you require your constant guidance, inspiration, and encouragement. You must motivate them into action and steer them toward the realization of your vision.

Among all Life Paths, you have the greatest potential for financial success, but it does demand effort and dedication.

8 Life Path

You have great talent for management in all areas of life, especially in business and financial matters. You understand the material world; you intuitively know what makes virtually any enterprise work.

Embracing the capacity to rebound from failures and defeats is vital, as you possess the resilience and character of a true survivor. It's not uncommon for those with an 8 Life Path to face significant setbacks, including financial downturns and bankruptcies. Nevertheless, you also wield the talent and sheer determination to amass more than one fortune and establish numerous prosperous ventures.

In the realm of marriage, your failures can be remarkably costly.

Despite life's hardships, you will find gratification in material wealth and the accompanying influence it brings. Fields such as business, finance, real estate, law, sciences (particularly history, archaeology, and physics), publishing, and the administration of sizable institutions are ideal vocational paths for you. Positions of influence and leadership naturally beckon to you, encompassing areas like politics, social work, and teaching, among numerous others where your abilities shine.

You possess an astute ability to assess character, aiding you in attracting the right individuals into your sphere. Most 8s tend to favor larger families, and their protective and sometimes somewhat authoritarian nature tempts them into occasionally prolonging the dependence of others longer than necessary.

Though your nature is jovial, you may not be overtly expressive in demonstrating love and affection. Your desire for opulence and comfort is notably strong, and status holds great importance. Vigilance is essential to avoid living beyond your means.

The 8 Life Path leads you into the delicate realm where power resides, and it has the potential to corrupt. There's a risk of becoming overly self-important, arrogant, and domineering, convinced that your path is the sole path. This path invariably leads to isolation and conflict, with those you cherish most—your family and friends—bearing the brunt.

Beware of transforming into a stubborn, intolerant, domineering, and impatient individual. These traits might emerge early in the life of an 8 Life Path, often arising from the experience of enduring a tyrannical parent or growing up in a family ensnared by oppressive religious or intellectual doctrines.

Individuals with the 8 Life Path typically boast robust physical constitutions, a testament to their inherent strength and resilience.

9 Life Path

The 9 Life Path embodies a spirit of philanthropy and humanitarianism. Individuals with a 9 Life Path are deeply attuned to social issues and harbor a profound concern for the state of the world, driven by their compassion and idealism.

You are a visionary, constantly striving to manifest some facet of your utopian dream throughout your life, willingly dedicating your time, energy, and resources to the betterment of humanity. The act of giving brings you immense satisfaction, and you possess a wide-ranging perspective on life, often focusing on the bigger picture rather than getting bogged down in minute details.

People from diverse backgrounds are naturally drawn to your inclusive plans, stepping in to handle areas you find less engaging. You eschew prejudice and social biases, choosing to evaluate individuals based on their potential contributions to the greater good. You are a true egalitarian.

As a 9 Life Path, you possess a vivid imagination and creativity, particularly when it comes to harmoniously enhancing the inherent beauty in your surroundings. Your talents can lead you into professions like interior decorating, landscape art, and photography. Given your strong social consciousness, you can also excel in roles such as politics, law, judgeship, ministry, teaching, healing, and environmental advocacy. You tend to gravitate toward vocations that demand self-sacrifice and have a clear societal impact.

You often experience disappointment with the realities of life, whether it's the shortcomings of others or your own. You have an innate desire to rectify imperfections in the world, and this relentless pursuit of improvement drives you constantly. However, you frequently find yourself unsatisfied with the results, lacking the perspective that could allow you to fully appreciate life and its inherent limitations. You possess controlled enthusiasm and the ability to see through your endeavors to completion.

Sacrifice is a central theme in your life. Learning to release material possessions and relationships is a key lesson, as you understand that clinging too tightly to anything ultimately causes pain. Money tends to come to you through unexpected avenues: perhaps an inheritance, the benevolence of someone inspired by your work, or a fortuitous investment.

Conversely, if you pursue money solely for its own sake, forsaking your larger aspirations, you may find yourself empty-handed. The most fulfilling path for a 9 involves giving, sharing, and sacrificing for a greater purpose, without expecting anything in return.

Your greatest potential for success lies in aligning your personal fortunes with endeavors that improve the world for others. Frequently, this leads to highly successful and lucrative ventures, amply providing for you and your loved ones. Your life philosophy centers around the idea that the more you give, the greater your rewards.

Your romantic inclinations tend to be more impersonal, as your focus often rests on your dreams. When out of sync with your true nature, you may experience moodiness, aloofness, and withdrawal. Timidity, uncertainty, and ingratitude can also surface, often with misplaced blame for your challenges directed toward others or the world.

You possess the remarkable ability to examine your life objectively from a certain distance, and honesty with yourself is your guiding principle. By openly acknowledging both your shortcomings and strengths, you attain equilibrium, enabling you to embrace yourself and all aspects of life with love and understanding.

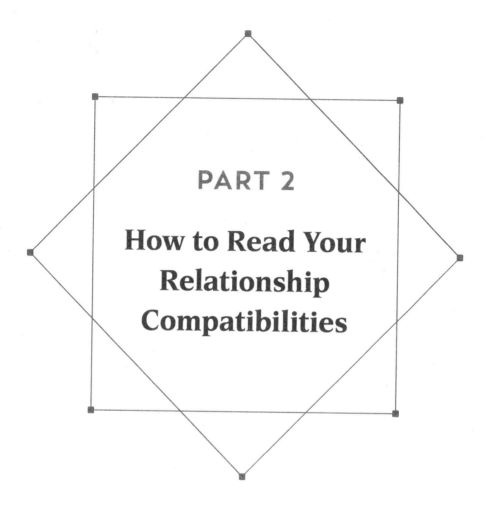

PART 2

How to Read Your Relationship Compatibilities

The first step in learning more about your compatibility with your partner is to calculate both of your Life Path numbers, and then familiarize yourself with the attributes you both possess. In the following pages, we will analyze each pairing. So, for example, if you have a 5 Life Path and your partner has an 8, look for the description of the Life Path for 5 and 8 as well as the one for 8 and 5, because while they obviously overlap, the description of each chapter is written from the point of view of the first person. In other words, the description for 5 and 8 would be from your perspective, while the chapter for 8 and 5 would be from your partner's perspective. You will notice they are similar, as they should be, since they are based on the same people, but the different perspectives are subtle and, hopefully, will help you and your partner relate to the strengths and weaknesses of your relationship.

You should also be aware that numerology is an inexact science and is meant only to help you understand your personalities from numerology's perspective. You should not take them as the final word but, rather, consider the possibilities and use your own powers of analysis to gain insight into your relationship.

Finally, you should know that there are other numbers in your chart that affect your relationship, but it is simply not possible to include all of them here. Your Life Path number is by far the most important of your numbers, which is why we've explored those in depth in this book.

CHAPTER 1

Life Path 1

Your partner is a 1

You make up a challenging and unusual combination. Most people with a 1 Life Path may befriend another 1 Life Path, but romance tends to be rare.

You are both headstrong and competitive, and neither one of you likes to play second fiddle. You are both unlikely to surrender your accustomed place at the top even to someone you are attracted to, and the result is that there will always be a competitive angle to the relationship. Most couples cherish the things they have in common, but in your case, that does not always translate into an advantage. Your shared personality traits can be quite disastrous if they are not recognized as such, and should be consciously avoided.

Your relationship is built on extremes, with powerful feelings and sometimes an urge to confront each other, which can easily escalate and create havoc within your relationship. When both partners have a 1 Life Path, their overbearing nature makes a tender, giving, cooperative relationship difficult. Both of you feel the need to be king of the mountain, and like bulls, you will butt heads to gain the upper hand.

However, if two strong-minded people with high energy drives can set aside their competitive natures—at least toward each other—the relationship becomes extraordinary in its loyalty and devotion to each other's happiness. Your relationship has a promise that is equal to its challenge, but it requires conscious effort to achieve this.

You should recognize the signs when one or both of you starts to push the other. You should have a plan to deal with those moments. Set rules, such as not to raise your voice, not to interrupt each other, and to hold hands, especially when you are in an argument—nothing works better to maintain harmony than a loving, physical touch. You might even consider a safe word; as soon as one of you utters it, stop talking, take a breath, and get in touch with those feelings that gave birth to your romance in the first place.

Remembering such rules in time, before the argument intensifies, is not easy. In fact, it is exceedingly difficult. However, if you are serious about your relationship, it will be your best defense against painful clashes and hurt feelings. You will both need to be willing to occasionally take second place.

Another potential challenge is that you are both independent and view relying on another person as a weakness—it is alien to your nature. You do things your way; you are not much for listening to others or accepting their advice. This can be a source of stress. The advice here is to practice humility and sensitivity, which, unfortunately, are not your strongest assets.

Finally, you both like to be in the forefront and the center of attention. This can cause friction when you find yourself at a social gathering, due to your penchant for outperforming each other. Fortunately, whereas most couples will work the room together, you each prefer to go it alone. If you do find you are competing for attention, one of you will need to muster the grace to let your partner have their moment.

But it is not all challenges and troubles. A powerful asset in a love relationship between two people with a 1 Life Path is that they want to protect and provide for each other. It is perhaps the most essential quality you share that can make this relationship last a lifetime.

One thing you do not have to worry about is that you might get bored with each other. You are both creative, curious, unconventional, and adventurous; you naturally learn and grow together. You stimulate each other, and if the challenges can be overcome, you will enrich each other tremendously. Your relationship truly is extraordinarily promising.

Your partner is a 2

You and your partner reside on opposite ends of the spectrum, and yet, the invisible bond of love is strong and may well last for many years, despite your differences in personalities and often practical issues, such as where to go on vacation or what kind of house to buy.

To you, more than to your partner, the difference in personality is a main source of attraction. You are not just drawn to them, you are intensely curious, as you sense a world, a reality, to which you are a stranger. You want to use your strength to protect them, because their gentleness makes you feel they are vulnerable, and you are there to make sure no harm will come to them. But you also tend to control and dominate, and sometimes the lines between a desire to protect and a need to control get blurred, and it can go from idyllic to bad quickly.

You are driven, ambitious, strong-willed, sometimes confrontational, and always ready to take the lead. Your partner is gentle, tactful, sensitive, intuitive, and not particularly troubled by playing the power behind the throne—and yes, you can be the one on the throne. Where you push, they give. Where you dominate, they surrender. Where you try to control, they accept. But make no mistake, this is not because you are stronger or more capable. It is because they are the water, whereas you are the boulder. They give in because they can, and they are not concerned about playing second fiddle. Your partner's strength and re-silience are dormant much of the time, but if provoked enough, their eyes throw daggers, and their words can cut even the loudest, most brutal opponent to ribbons.

It is precisely owing to your directly opposite Life Paths that you have such a powerful and potentially rewarding attraction to each other. Your strength is less complicated and certainly less reserved, and it is a powerful asset in your life. You will go places and forcefully make progress. You tend not to take no for an answer, and when motivated, you are able to overcome just about any obstacle. Your partner is your perfect complement and together you are a formidable couple.

Of course, the essential differences between you and your partner can also cause friction, but these moments tend to be trivial and short-lived, in large part because of your partner's ability and willingness to bend. Your partner is more patient and always conscious of the bigger picture. Diplomatic, intuitive, insightful, and supportive, they will usually allow you to assume the more assertive role while discreetly making sure the job gets done.

The fact that you do not vie for power is key in this relationship. Both of you know and understand your wants and needs and, in your own way, can express them to each other. Being comfortable in the roles you have chosen helps you complement each other well.

There are no Life Path numbers as paradoxical as the 1 and the 2. They truly are on opposite ends of the spectrum. Your partner is the peacemaker, and you are the driving, ambitious force. For that reason, you will need to be careful with your partner's sensitive nature. Your strength is like a strong stick—you will not break easily, and you are not all that concerned with getting hurt. Your partner's strength is more flexible, but also more vulnerable. Your partner is sensitive to harsh words and criticism and will surrender more easily but is also surprisingly resilient; like the shape of the number 2 suggests, you can force it down, but when the pressure lets up, it will spring right back to its original shape.

It is precisely because your partner can bend that your partner is likely to be the survivor if a major storm hits, whereas, if the wind is strong enough, your strength may snap. You may be able to shrug off judgment or criticism from others without much damage to your ego, but if enough pressure is applied, you could break.

It may seem a contradiction, but your partner's flexibility and resilience are the qualities that will help you overcome difficulties, such as emotional distress or anxiety, troubles that cannot be fixed with the strength and personal power that are the typical traits of your 1 Life Path, while your partner benefits on many levels from your drive, courage, and determination. It is, in many ways, a perfect fit.

Your partner is a 3

You are fortunate to have formed one of the most harmonious combinations for a happy, pleasurable, long-lasting relationship. Your individualism and originality, typical of a 1, combined with the creativity and "anything goes" attitude of your partner's 3 Life Path, creates an exciting and often adventurous relationship. You play together, laugh together, and likely have inspirational and enlightening conversations.

The characteristics that are the essence of your 1 Life Path make you the central force in this relationship, while your partner contributes by bringing the sunshine and lightness of heart that will help the two of you deal with obstacles more easily than most couples.

Despite the unusual number of positive aspects in this combination, you should be on the alert for potential pitfalls. You value responsibility and loyalty and have a natural ability to put forth sustained effort in pursuit of goals and dreams.

Your partner is more playful, creative, and restless, and changes direction quickly, especially if a goal seems difficult to reach, which can be frustrating for you. Paradoxically, it is precisely these differences that bring balance to your relationship.

You should be aware that you can be quite stubborn and hardheaded, which can cause your partner considerable emotional stress. If you experience discord in the relationship, you should take a close look at your attitude and consider if your unwillingness to bend might be a contributing factor to the disharmony.

All in all, there are very few negative influences with this combination of Life Paths. Still, it is important to keep an eye on potential challenges, continue to fully explore your respective natural qualities, and enjoy a happy, enriching, and rewarding life together for many years. You have the potential to develop your relationship to near perfection.

Your partner is a 4

There are enough traits you and your partner have in common to give this relationship a good start and a solid foundation. However, you also have qualities that are conflicting and likely to cause problems.

You are a strong-willed, highly motivated self-starter and an unconventional individualist. You are adventurous and ready to try anything new, even risky endeavors. People with a 1 Life Path are not usually concerned about other people's expectations; they march to their own drums. Your partner, however, is made from a vastly different cloth.

Your partner is equally persistent and ambitious but has an entirely different approach. The 4, your partner's Life Path number, is solid, reliable, patient, responsible, conventional, detail-oriented, and "does things the right way."

Both of you are strong-willed and ambitious, but you are highly independent, unconventional, and individualistic, while your partner is a team player, rather conventional, and generally willing to conform to society's norms and other people's expectations. This difference is precisely where potential pitfalls lie in your relationship.

Your partner has both feet planted firmly on the ground. Undeterred by the prospect of dealing with things that are boring or routine, your partner will complete the job no matter what. You, on the other hand, do not have that kind of patience and will barge ahead, not as concerned about the consequences as you probably should be.

Your relationship can thrive unless you start down a path of unknowns with risky, questionable aims. This is likely to happen at times, at which point your partner will seem like a stick-in-the-mud and a source of frustration for you. If this conflict is not handled with care, it could bring an end to the relationship. Your Life Paths' combination of 1 and 4 can be as solid as a rock for a long period of time, only to crash and burn in an instant.

However, if you can respect your partner's need for a secure, predictable lifestyle, and your partner can understand your need to try new things and occasionally venture into the unknown, the relationship could endure. The key is in understanding and accepting each other's differences.

Your partner is a 5

This relationship is based on one of the most promising and exciting combinations possible, with potentially ecstatic experiences of love, spiritual bonding, and shared dreams. It is also one that even during the best of times tends to exist close to the edge, which is a major cause of the attraction, as both of you are drawn to risk and adventure.

Neither you nor your partner are happy staying in a safe zone for long; change and new experiences drive you both, but for different reasons. You are always looking for what is around the next corner, a deeply ingrained need to get there first, to be the spearhead. Your partner is the adventurer, someone who needs change and thrives on the unexpected. It is, in many ways, a match made in heaven. There will rarely be boredom, complacency, or emptiness in a relationship that has heads turning and people whispering.

However, yours is a relationship of extremes; your different yet generally compatible personality traits have the potential to create or destroy. At their best, the 1 and the 5 are like a thoroughbred and its rider; when they work in harmony, nothing can stop them, but if you are not in harmony, someone could get hurt. When you and your partner clash, it is a fearful thing to watch. You are both passionate and easily consumed by real or imagined slights or injustice. Compromise does not come naturally to you or your partner, and you are both willing to cut off your nose to spite your face. Your pride is your greatest handicap, you tend to view compromise as a weakness, and unless you are willing to let it go and humble yourself, the first major clash will also be the last.

Your partner knows your strength and is, deep down, a little afraid of it. They know that getting you to back down is like facing down a lion.

Your partner, unlikely as it may seem, is the stronger one in your relationship, at least when it means survival and walking away from a bad experience relatively unscathed. This is due to their great capacity to accept change, to be flexible, and to detach. Your partner can be hurt, but they get over it quicker than most people, and their innate faith in their ability to find another path, another partner, to adjust to a new life, helps them move on. You, on the other hand, once broken, will need more time and are more likely to be badly damaged.

That said, you and your partner are well equipped to prevent that kind of devastation by turning toward your softer side. A conscious effort to deny yourself the satisfaction of "winning" the argument and instead bow down and reach out—the emotional equivalent of kissing their hand and telling them they are the most beautiful thing you have ever seen in your life—is the most powerful healing lotion in the world.

Unfortunately, that is not your natural approach to confrontations, so you will need to do what does not come easily and learn that there is often more strength in surrender than in persevering.

As for your partner, their tendency to just drop it and move on when faced with a painful confrontation can become a source of regret. Your partner may heal quickly, but they do not forget, and it can haunt them.

You can have a romantic relationship most couples can only dream of, full of passion and delight, filled with adventure, enriching both of you, and proving that indeed the sum is more than its parts. For that reason, the effort needed to prevent the kind of confrontation that can break such a promising romance should be constant and conscious. When that is the case, your relationship is safe even through turbulent times.

Your partner is a 6

Yours is truly a lovely combination. Your partner's 6 represents the most harmonious of all numbers, with a great capacity for love, understanding, sacrifice, and support. Your strong, dynamic 1 reflects the ability and desire to protect and defend your partner through thick and thin, making them feel safe and secure. This is a combination that can last for a long time without the turbulence so many relationships experience. But, as always, there is another side to the coin.

You have an inner determination and a dynamic energy that does not slow down for anything. You do not look kindly on weakness and can be demanding of others. Your partner recognizes the leader in you, and as such expects courage and strength to be always there. Your partner is different: compromising, forgiving, and sometimes self-sacrificing. You should be careful not to see this as a weakness, because it is not. Your partner has no problem taking a back seat to you or others, but when the need arises, they can display great strength and courage. The danger in this relationship is that you may be tempted to underestimate your partner. No relationship can be harmonious and mutually satisfying if one partner disrespects the other.

Another potential challenge is that your partner may at times be disturbed by the somewhat gruff and unforgiving quality you can display. Your partner should not confuse this with a lack of compassion. You are quite capable of feeling empathy toward victims of circumstances in which negligence, laziness, or cowardice is not the cause. However, you have difficulty feeling sympathy for those who display such weaknesses, for they are simply unacceptable to you. In the eyes of your partner, our flawed, weaker brothers and sisters are precisely those who need our help and sympathy the most. Your partner may be dismayed by your harsh and critical attitude toward those you consider weak, and the truth is, you would greatly benefit if you could become a little more forgiving and less judgmental, that is, more like your partner. After all, the feeling of empathy and love toward others, especially those who are troubled and in need of help, is equally rewarding to the giver and the recipient.

The important thing for both of you to recognize is that you sometimes differ in your opinions about what the most valuable human qualities are. If you can respect this contrast and value each other's positive qualities, your relationship has the potential to be happy and long-lasting.

Your partner is a 7

The initial attraction in this combination is usually intellectual, because that is where you relate and have plenty to share. But that does not mean you have a lot in common, or a similar attitude toward, well, just about anything. You are very different people, and those differences are either experienced as exciting and compatible, giving spice and depth to the relationship, or they can cause major conflict, quickly and almost without warning. For that reason, while your Life Path combination has a powerful potential connection, it can be explosive.

It is likely that your partner, who is intensely curious and challenges things most of us take for granted, realized at an early age that others thought them peculiar and offbeat. Your partner's perspective was often unique and quite advanced for a young person, which made them stand apart from the crowd and possibly caused them to be bullied or made to feel inept. This sense of being different and not able to relate is part of the reason your partner is attracted to you. Your unorthodox and often brazen attitude toward traditional concepts, your willingness to get off the beaten path, and your open and unconventional mind is a suitable companion to your partner's uniquely imaginative and spiritual view of the world.

Your attitudes differ, however, in the way you approach life—you in a somewhat aggressive, confrontational way, your partner in a usually quiet, introspective manner. Your relationship benefits from the fact that you are both happy to venture into new, strange, or unknown intellectual and spiritual territories. You are both free thinkers, but in different ways. You tend to be in the forefront, modern and innovative. Your partner keeps digging and searching and isn't satisfied until their understanding feels right and complete. Your differing perspectives create a spicy, captivating relationship that forms the basis for an almost unbreakable bond. But that does not mean your relationship is free of challenges.

It is in matters of the heart—feelings and emotions—where you might encounter trouble spots. Neither of you is eager to expose your inner self. Both of you are emotionally reclusive, sensitive, and vulnerable and do not wear your heart on your sleeve. You recognize strength and endurance as your inborn assets and abhor even the slightest perception of weakness in yourself. Your partner is more comfortable dwelling in their inner world of thought rather than feelings.

To help your relationship grow on the deepest level, you will need emotional courage. Allow yourself to be open, sensitive, receptive, and vulnerable. This requires faith in your partner, but, more important, faith in yourself. Both of you, but particularly your partner, may be tempted to go the other way, to become cynical and find refuge in sarcasm.

Without a conscious appreciation of feelings, no relationship can survive. Therefore, welcome your feelings even if it feels awkward or confusing, and share them. Allow yourself to be vulnerable—your relationship will be the stronger for it.

Your partner is an 8

The 1 Life Path and the 8 Life Path have much in common, and that, my friend, is a double-edged sword. Your respective numbers make you both strong-willed with a tendency to dominate those around you. This combination often feels like there are two captains on the ship, and their conflicting viewpoints can lead to discomfort or even explosive arguments. A willingness to compromise is extremely important for your relationship.

This combination is generally more suitable for a business relationship than a romantic one, but if there is a romance between the two of you, being involved in a shared business or other venture will almost certainly strengthen your personal relationship.

You both have good business instincts. Your partner most likely has the greater talent for managing financial affairs, while you tend to be the engine, the driving force behind any project. Should you decide to work together, make sure to keep your responsibilities separate to avoid potential conflicts.

Whether in business or your personal lives, you will need to have faith in each other's abilities and respect your independence. With both of you preferring to do things your own way, this may not be an easy task. Neither of you allows the other to take charge, nor do you feel comfortable as the other's sidekick. You also have different priorities; your partner's is seeing tangible results and reward, while you are more interested in the satisfaction that comes from the accomplishment of reaching a goal. However, if mutual trust and faith are the basis of your work relationship, your personal and romantic relationship will be almost unbreakable.

A word of caution: You both tend to be quite direct; tact and diplomacy are not your strong suits. You can be confrontational and argumentative, especially when things are not going to your liking. You must be careful not to take it out on your partner, something you may be tempted to do because they give an impression of strength. This is an illusion; your partner will hear the anger, frustration, or blame in the tone of your voice and be deeply hurt without showing it, and that can do lasting damage. Your partner is not one to show their sensitive side, so they hide it and allow it to fester until, one day, they simply turn around and walk away.

While you are both good in business, which requires communication skills, you do not communicate well when it comes to personal issues. You both must agree to talk, and talk carefully, deliberately, and honestly. Sharing feelings and a willingness to compromise are key to your relationship, and unfortunately, you do not compromise easily. This is the single biggest threat to your relationship; if you cannot compromise, your romance will not last.

Your partner is a 9

The 1 Life Path and the 9 Life Path are at opposite ends of the spectrum and have profoundly conflicting influences. While opposites often tend to attract each other, you and your partner are so diametrically different that it may be too much to overcome, especially in the long run, as there is little common ground.

Relationships with this combination tend to have a short, passion-ate, and almost certainly turbulent love affair, but it rarely lasts. People are likely to find you and your partner in this romantic relationship puzzling—together, yet so different from each other.

There are exceptions, of course, usually due to other numbers in your numerology chart that bridge the gaps and strengthen the bond. When that is the case, the first year or two will most likely still be ex-ceedingly difficult, but if you and your partner have been in a romantic relationship for three or more years, you have proven that the power of love can overcome even extreme differences.

At the core of the challenge between your conflicting personalities is an inability to relate to each other; you quite literally view your worlds from opposite ends. For your partner, everything is measured and un-derstood based on how their actions affect others, while for you every-thing depends on how your actions reflect on you. This is not selflessness versus selfishness but, rather, whether you experience life as if looking in a mirror or through a window.

Even if your relationship survives the first couple of years, you will likely still clash regularly, but there is much you can do to overcome these challenges. You need to respect each other, give each other room to be your own person, and strive to find common ground. Where most relationships benefit from a close connection and an intimately shared environment, yours will be more successful if you have a clearly defined and separate space.

Neither of you conforms easily to the rules and expectations of soci-ety, which is one of the few characteristics you share. You are more of an avant-garde, modern person with little or no desire to play by other peo-ple's rules. You get off the beaten path and like to do things differently. Your partner is equally nonconformist, but their motivations are likely rooted in idealism. It is not uncommon for a 9 to embrace a lifestyle that is both unconventional and driven by a desire to make a positive impact on the world. For example, they may become involved in alternative health practices, or they might be passionate about supporting ethical consumerism, advocating for the purchase of handmade goods from developing countries to promote fair trade and uplift artisans. Their choices tend to reflect a commitment to values that prioritize sustainability, social justice, and the betterment of society.

You are both creative, but again, it is expressed differently. You invent and create; you are quite original. Your partner will tend to work with existing objects and materials, to mix them and create something new. You may even have discussed a shared creative venture, and if that is the case, it has a good chance of being successful.

Still, the bottom line is that you view life and your world from quite different angles, which makes sharing ideas and thoughts both more important and more difficult. You would do well putting in conscious effort to listen to your partner without interrupting or thinking about a response. Be open, and you can learn a lot and widen your perspective by listening to your partner.

CHAPTER 2

Life Path 2

Your partner is a 1

Although you have very little in common, this is a promising combination. The personalities and character traits of the 1 Life Path and the 2 Life Path are quite literally on opposite ends of the spectrum. Where your partner's strength and power reside on the surface of their personality, yours is buried within you, hiding behind a gentle exterior. Where your gentle, sensitive, and sympathetic nature is clearly visible to all, your partner's gentle side is hidden behind a more boisterous facade—exposing itself only when their heart is deeply touched.

You are drawn to your partner because you are attracted to their strength, determination, loyalty, power, ambition, and courage. You see and appreciate the bravura they often display, but you know quite well that it is nothing more than a way to assert their space and territory.

You are sensitive and gentle, and your intuition is extremely well developed, allowing you to recognize the vulnerable, softer core underneath their forceful exterior, and it touches you deeply. In fact, sensing their vulnerability under such a warrior-like exterior is incredibly attractive to you.

But there are potential pitfalls. Your partner is competitive, and likely somewhat domineering. You are the opposite; the need for peace and harmony are central to your nature. You are tactful, delicate, insightful, supportive, and calm. You have no desire to be confrontational or overly assertive, but make no mistake—this does not mean you are weak or cowardly. You know your deeper, inner strength, and this gives you the confidence to accept a role that may appear almost compliant to the casual observer but is simply your way to give your partner the space and confidence they need to be comfortable. You are the power behind the throne and don't mind your partner taking the limelight and occupying that throne, because you know full well that your partner needs you—more, perhaps, than you need them. You allow your partner to assume the more dominant role, while you quietly make sure things are done your way.

The fact that you do not vie for power is key to the success of this relationship. Both of you know your wants and needs and, in your own way, can express them to each other. Being comfortable in the roles you have chosen helps you to complement each other well. However, it is important to look at other compatible aspects to keep everything in perspective. Your partner must be careful with your sensitive nature. They can be tactless and confrontational; they are the proverbial bull in the china shop when it comes to delicate issues. Your strength is more flexible and resilient; you are a true survivor, whereas your partner will struggle and fight to their limit, but when they reach it, it's game over for them. You, on the other hand, will rise back up over and over, as long as it takes.

When you are in an argument, your partner will not bend easily; they are hardheaded and feel that admitting they are wrong makes them weak and vulnerable. Harsh words and criticism will seem to affect you more, but the truth is that your partner is equally harmed—even if they refuse to show it. Hurting their pride can do lasting damage. And although you are the sensitive one in this relationship, given some time, you can shrug off judgment or criticism from others without lasting damage, because you do not suffer from pride as much as your partner.

When push comes to shove and times are difficult and turbulent, you will be the stronger one because you bend and adapt more easily. Your partner's considerable strength and personal power can withstand a lot, but they will snap eventually.

The key to a healthy relationship between such opposite personalities is mutual respect and acceptance of your differences. Your partner needs to understand that your willingness to compromise or surrender does not indicate weakness or an indecisive nature. Your partner should also be aware that you are not easily fooled. Although you may accept an explanation or situation without confrontation, it is due to your intuition and your tolerance that you forgive quickly, most certainly not cowardice. And you should keep in mind that your partner's displays of bravado and confidence do not mean they are not susceptible to hurt feelings. As you probably already know, behind that facade is someone who experiences matters of the heart deeply, and their loyalty and desire to protect you are second to none. They are the hard shell and soft inner core, while you are the soft exterior and strong inner core. This makes for a powerful alliance and a relationship that can weather many storms.

Your partner is a 2

This is a rare and somewhat challenging combination among romantic partners. Identical numbers are not usually attracted to each other romantically; they can be friends for life, but romance is rare. As a rule of thumb, those with a 2 Life Path tend to be attracted to one of the more forceful, masculine numbers such as 1, 4, or 8. But when a person with a 2 is attracted to another 2 and vice versa, at least one of you has experienced hard lessons, likely had a difficult childhood, and has learned to be more assertive and forceful than came naturally.

If, against the odds, two people who both have a 2 Life Path do fall in love, it tends to be quite an intense roller-coaster ride full of ups and downs due to the extremely sensitive nature of a 2. You are both highly susceptible to emotional turmoil, which can cause an otherwise minor drama to be magnified out of proportion. It is important that you guard against making mountains out of molehills.

Another challenge is that a troubling situation can arise when you are both experiencing sadness and are looking for emotional support, because instead of empowering and uplifting each other, you may find that you weaken each other. Under those circumstances, one of you needs to be strong and decisive, ignore their own troubles, and take control. Fortunately, the 2 has a surprisingly powerful and strong inner core that even people close to you may not be aware of; their resilience is legendary. A 2 Life Path can display calm determination when the fight is less driven by emotion than by their empathy and sense of justice, usually when they are protecting someone else.

Both of you are highly emotional, but when dealing with the suffering or troubles of others, you can be calm and controlled. It is not uncommon for a 2 to step into a turbulent, even violent skirmish and confront the most threatening force, standing tall and strong, until even the loudest bully backs down. You are the peacemaker for a reason, and it is not always displayed by your tact and diplomacy. You are both capable of making yourselves the buffer between a violator and a victim.

You and your partner tend to experience other people's criticism or general negativity more intensely than most people, and this is both a positive and a negative asset in your relationship. This is because you are somewhat dramatic by nature and inclined to play the victim and respond by being passive-aggressive or giving the other the silent treatment. On the upside, you can sense your partner's emotional state of mind quite accurately, and if you can find it in your heart to forgive, you can reach out and use your considerable diplomatic skills to resolve the issue.

Finally, the negative side of a 2 Life Path is a willingness to bend the truth or straight-out lie. And it can therefore be expected that you are also quite capable of recognizing a lie when you hear one—the 2 picks up on subtle signs that escape most other people, so lying to your partner will usually backfire.

The key to maintaining a healthy relationship when both partners have a 2 Life Path is to recognize the need for heart-to-heart talks that are consciously and purposely meant to be therapeutic, to heal, not just to overcome differences or resolve arguments. The 2 is a natural-born counselor, so use it in your relationship; take turns to counsel and comfort each other—it will do wonders for your relationship. You may even want to schedule these chats on a regular basis, like once a week. Create a setting: make a cup of tea or pour a glass of wine, sit in comfortable surroundings, and begin by confirming your love and commitment. Respect, care, and direct, honest communication will help you form a deep, long-lasting relationship.

Your partner is a 3

You and your partner are both creative, but in different ways. Your sense of beauty, good taste, and inborn need for symmetry inspires you to beautify anything you touch. Your partner's creativity is more playful, unconventional, and imaginative. Creativity is the underlying basis of your relationship, even if it is not particularly obvious. You are attracted to the childlike joy and the easy way your partner can find happiness in small things. Your partner is impressed by the grace and sense of depth they see in you. It is a beautiful, passionate romance, and yet also always a little on the edge.

Sensitive, intuitive, gentle, and tactful, you are made of different cloth than your straightforward, loose-lipped, happy-go-lucky, and probably somewhat irresponsible partner. For you, life is serious. For your partner, it is a play that should be enjoyed. This difference can cause superficial but damaging issues.

With the sensitive 2 as your number, you may find it difficult to handle criticism and confrontation, which has the potential to make you hold grudges and become resentful—and occasionally find refuge in a white lie. Your partner is quite different, as they allow negative comments to roll off without doing much harm. This does not mean your partner cannot be hurt but simply that your partner does not allow such relatively minor things to spoil the day.

By the same token, your partner does not always realize that a comment they made hurts you deeply. This is not because your partner is insensitive and inconsiderate, although they certainly can be, but more often because they have difficulty accepting that someone could be so sensitive and easily hurt. Your response, therefore, should be to speak up right away. Unfortunately, speaking up is not your forte. As a result, even minor issues can grow into big emotional dramas.

While your partner tends to be less affected by criticism or an emotional exchange, they also have less control over their feelings—consider it due to a lack of practice. This might lead to expressing increasingly angry and sharp words. You might respond with a few angry words too but will more likely just withdraw. If this happens, a kernel of resentment can develop and sometimes remain hidden for a long time. This should be recognized and handled before it becomes so large and intense that it can permanently damage your relationship.

When your emotions become overbearing, you lose the ability to view your disagreements rationally or objectively. In response, your partner may feel helpless and become discontented to the point that they too will turn their back on the relationship. While this seems a rather negative and disheartening view of your relationship, it is meant to make you realize the importance of taking care of disagreements early on. You must overcome your dislike of confrontations and be willing to step up and make yourself heard, calmly and with clarity. If you feel you cannot do that, write your feelings on paper. Read and edit them, then sit down with your partner close enough to hold hands, and start talking.

On a more positive note, the combination of 2 and 3 can be extraordinarily strong and long-term, especially if your partner keeps verbal impulses under control and you have enough self-confidence to handle occasional criticism.

The sense of harmony and rhythm associated with the 2 merges beautifully with the creative powers of expression so natural to the 3. Your relationship can be strengthened enormously by sharing creative interests and has every chance of bringing love and joy into your life. Beauty and love are the foundation of your relationship. The key to weathering your differences is to discuss issues openly, frankly, and with tact and sensitivity as soon as they arise.

Your partner is a 4

Your partner is the rock you can lean on. Their reliable, trustworthy, solid personality suits you well, while they are strongly attracted to your gentle, intuitive, and sensitive qualities. You are different, but quite compatible. In fact, this is one of the best combinations for business too. You are people-oriented, and you can maintain harmony in any environment where people interact, whether in a family, a social setting, or a workplace. Human resources is a natural fit for a 2 Life Path. Your partner is pragmatic, detail-oriented, systematic, decisive, disciplined, and highly rational, but prefers to work with matter, whether it is graphs, tools, instruments, or materials. They are happier if they can predict and plan the results without having to rely on the whims of human beings. You are water, they are earth; together you can build something impressive.

These same qualities also form a good foundation for a romantic relationship. You easily share duties and keep your roles separate. Fortunately, your partner is anything but a slacker, so you can count on them to share the chores. Your partner also has good parenting skills, and this is another area where you complement each other well. They will handle discipline, order, and set the boundaries, while you can be the gentle, softer touch. It is a promising combination for a family.

There are some qualities that can cause problems. Your partner can be rude and tactless—not out of malice but because they are not as emotionally vulnerable and sensitive as you are and do not realize the harshness of their words. This is perhaps your biggest challenge for this relationship, to accept that your partner is not as in touch with their emotions as you are, and that you need to grow a thick skin. Their sometimes tactless remarks have nothing to do with a lack of love or respect, and there is no malice. However, they can be angered rather easily, and while they have reasonable self-control, they can be pushed over the edge. When a 4 gets angry, they can be cold and fierce, and it will take time for them to calm down. They are not usually violent, but they will hold a grudge, and it will be up to you to use your considerable diplomatic skills to calm them down and help them get past it.

You are subtle, and guided mostly by feelings, and your partner is practical and tends to be more rational—this can occasionally cause discord, but in general, it is a combination that brings balance to the relationship, strengthening and complementing both of you. Like mortar and bricks, yours is one of the best possible combinations and could potentially weather even the most turbulent times.

Your partner is a 5

When a 2 Life Path and a 5 Life Path connect, they have the potential to produce a powerful and memorable but sometimes short-lived relationship. The initial attraction is strong and passionate. You see someone who has all the qualities you fear but also excite you: 5s are impulsive, daring, dynamic. Your partner is the kind of person who will take chances, and if something does not work out, they shrug it off and move on. There is a kind of detachment, a carelessness you wish you had. Your partner looks at you and sees someone who feels strongly, who is guided by love and intuition, and who always tries to bring harmony and comfort to their environment and to others. Your partner wants and admires what you have, and you want and admire what they have. Based on that, your relationship should be an easy and lasting one. Unfortunately, there are some differences in your personalities that are rather challenging.

On a deeper level, you have difficulty relating to each other; you sometimes just do not get where your partner is coming from. You are sensitive and strongly affected by your emotions; your feelings guide you. You make friends easily and have a wide circle of people you love and whose company you enjoy. If love is the gravity that binds us, your gravity is stable and strong. Your partner is driven by a need for freedom, for change, for excitement, and their gravity is more likely to sling them from one universe to another. After some time, you might get impatient with your partner's lack of stability and predictability, which may seem to you synonymous with being unreliable, but that is not true. Your partner is a 5, and despite their restless nature, they are extremely loyal. It may appear a contradiction, because they have a dynamic nature and love change, but when it comes to romance, they are the least likely Life Path number to cheat.

Yours can be a strong, lifelong relationship if you accept each other as you are; to acknowledge and appreciate your differences and be able to live side by side, yet also somewhat independently. Focus on the things you have in common and give each other plenty of room in areas of contention. Do your best to understand your partner, but do not expect to fully grasp their way of thinking.

Your partner is a 6

The 2 Life Path and the 6 Life Path are considered the most loving numbers of all. However, they express their love in different ways. Your 2 reveals your sensitivity, your emotional awareness of yourself and others, and your ability to read the subtle and often hidden motives in others. You are highly intuitive and feel strongly; your emotions rule your life. Your partner was born with a powerful urge to comfort, care for, and protect others. In fact, one of the few traits a 6 must guard against is smothering others with their love.

This combination forms a strong foundation for a romantic relationship. You both surrender to your romantic side easily and without reservation, and neither of you is afraid to reveal your feelings. However, it is only in the strength of your love and your need to give that these numbers overlap. In many other respects, you are quite different, and sometimes even opposites. Your love focus is driven by the need for companionship, security, and comfort. You are intuitively aware of the fragile nature of life and likely tend to be a little needy and perhaps somewhat insecure. This has the potential to produce jealousy about your partner's friends or business associates. Your partner, on the other hand, can be oblivious to the subtle signs that something is brewing under your quiet demeanor. Your partner is less likely to feel insecure in the relationship and does not consider spending time with others a sign that the romance is weakening.

Although your partner is not particularly afraid of romantic competition and is not the jealous type, their weak spots also show up in this relationship. Where you require attention and emotional support to be comfortable and secure, your partner tends to spread attention around and thrives on the approval and appreciation from others. Although sincere, your partner may reach out to care and comfort others to fill a space that cannot be filled, sometimes forgetting to focus on what (or who) is more important.

Most likely, neither of these issues will seriously threaten your relationship; the two of you are highly compatible, certainly more than most number combinations. Being aware of your differences, talking about them, and respecting them in each other can help you form a rewarding, long-lasting relationship.

Your partner is a 7

In this combination of numbers, intuition meets intelligence, sensitivity meets logic, and the heart meets the mind. It would be a challenge to find two more different archetypes than yours. You have a surprising relationship; rarely do people with such different characteristics express even the slightest interest in each other, but when they do, their romance is worth the effort. You almost certainly met under unusual circumstances, perhaps when you were both outside your normal environment, and it is likely you are the one who initially reached out to your partner. You may have had to overcome your partner's barrier of awkwardness and shyness, but once these dissimilar personalities get close enough, the result is often an exchange of energy that welds a romance for life.

Potential pitfalls in this combination are generally experienced at the beginning of the relationship. There tend to be many challenges, including the inability to relate to your partner's way of thinking, feeling, or expressing emotion—something they are simply not particularly good at. They prefer to analyze, not dwell on feelings. They sometimes hide their feelings behind cynicism and sarcasm, but don't think they cannot be emotional. On the contrary, they feel deeply, and their actions are often motivated by empathy, but rather than display their feelings, they take a rational, pragmatic approach. Your way of expressing love is soft and gentle, idealistic, romantic, emotional, and innocently childlike. Your partner is less emotional and expressive—like a precious jewel, their love requires a great deal of effort to earn.

At the onset of the relationship, your partner's reluctance to express their emotions was probably the biggest hurdle to overcome. They are not likely to trust love that comes easily, while you question why something as natural as love should be so difficult to communicate.

Sometimes, a relationship with this combination occurs after the partners have known each other for some time, when trust and understanding have been established and before either of you considered a romantic relationship. A romance based on a balance, of feelings on one side and mental and spiritual understanding on the other, has a good chance of lasting a lifetime.

Your partner is an 8

You are drawn to your partner in large part because they have great inner strength and the kind of personal power and self-confidence that often leads to success. Capable and goal-oriented, your partner is a force to be reckoned with.

You experience life on many levels, and you know the heart and understand the power of emotions. Your partner is attracted to you largely because they recognize in you an emotional and spiritual wealth that has likely remained dormant in their own life, at least to some extent. When brought together, the innate qualities of the 2 Life Path and the 8 Life Path can produce a rewarding, balanced relationship, as you complement each other extremely well.

This is a combination with the potential to survive long-term. However, there is also the possibility of miscalculating your strength as a couple. You must be careful that the relationship between you and your partner is not based on the assumption that your partner will never change. You admire your partner's strength and believe it will always be there. Your partner is attracted to your romantic, emotional nature and expects it to be unwavering. But there will be times when their strength will falter, and you should be prepared to be there for them and not to let disappointment create resentment. You must be alert and responsive to each other and not allow issues to fester.

Every couple must accept the changing nature of relationships as they ebb and flow over time. The key to success in yours is to recognize each other as whole, complex individuals, seeing beyond your first impression and your partner's most distinctive characteristics. You must respect and accept your partner's weaknesses as well as their strengths and abilities. Your partner needs to realize that there is more to you than the gentle, romantic, accommodating partner they fell in love with.

Few combinations tend to give birth to relationships based on misperception as often as the 2 and the 8. You both have many other qualities to bring to your relationship. Combine your respective strengths and you should have a rewarding, long-lasting relationship.

Your partner is a 9

You are open and relatively easygoing in matters of the heart, but your partner tends to be more careful and perhaps somewhat distant, even aloof. Your partner tends to maintain a distance, at times a coolness, that can be unsettling and confusing to you (as it has almost certainly been with previous relationships they were involved in).

On one hand, they will indicate their romantic interest in ways that are undeniable, through gifts and paying attention; they are considerate, generous, and protective. This is in part to hide their inherent reluctance to show affection or express their love in more romantic and physical ways.

You are fortunate to have the qualities of a 2, because gaining their love and their trust requires your sensitivity and finely tuned radar, as you gently and patiently probe their heart and try to get past their barriers. They are skittish because they know they are not well equipped to deal with heartbreaks. Trying to get them to be romantically involved is a little like inviting someone with a fear of heights to join you on the balcony of a high-rise; they will be on full alert and backing off when they feel they are too close to the edge.

You are the opposite—you are willing to take a chance and allow yourself to be vulnerable almost from day one. You can be spontaneous and generous in your expressions of love. The intimacy and physical expression of love comes naturally to you. You are affectionate and you need to feel their touch, literally and figuratively. Your partner is more inhibited, and probably always will be, but once they surrender to the love they feel, they are there to stay. Your partner's loyalty and selfless support become your rock.

It is easier for you, and you should therefore be the guide to take your partner to a place where they are comfortable sharing their deepest feelings without hesitation. When you reach that place, your partner's commitment and devotion will be strong and clear and obvious. But even then, there will be moments when your partner backs away when you least expect it; do not let that discourage you. The 9 is always looking for a wider perspective, even in their romantic relationships. Your partner's occasional need for distance does not mean their love is less real or not as strong as yours.

As a rule of thumb, when romance is not part of the picture, the 2 Life Path and 9 Life Path do not get along easily and are not usually friends. Although both numbers are caring, loving numbers, your love is aimed at the people around you, whether at home, in a social setting, or in the workplace, whereas the idealistic 9 prefers to focus on the world at large, on strangers and issues concerning humanity, often in a pragmatic and self-sacrificing way.

Interestingly, the 2 and the 9 sometimes form powerful alliances in other circumstances, such as business or institutions, where they complement each other well and can work together without the need for bonding. It is not uncommon for a romantic partnership between a 2 and a 9 to also include a successful business.

CHAPTER 3

Life Path 3

Your partner is a 1

This is one of the most harmonious and potentially enriching relationships possible. Your creative, somewhat happy-go-lucky attitude fits well with your more serious, ambitious, and go-getting partner. You are optimistic by nature, which is a blessing in any relationship, but with the more driven, determined numbers, such as your partner's, it is especially helpful. Your naturally sunny disposition offers your sometimes anxious and easily frustrated partner great relief.

However, your upbeat, lighthearted, and almost childlike mindset can also backfire when you let it distract you from goals and responsibilities, or when you let yourself too easily off the hook by giving up on a project or a venture when the going gets tough. This is almost certainly a touchy area for your partner, as they take responsibility and stay the course, even under difficult circumstances, which they see as a requirement and a source of pride. Your partner may see you at times as weak, and in their eyes, that is almost unforgivable. If you want to make your relationship strong and lasting, you must up your game and be more disciplined and goal-oriented. These are qualities you should strive for, regardless of your relationship, as they do not come easily to a 3 Life Path.

You are unconventional, as is your partner. When you're together in a social or formal environment, you are noticed, and people tend to enjoy your company—as a couple, you impress, and this can open doors in turn. You often inspire people, while your partner's leadership qualities shine through and draw respect. However, you will find that those attractive qualities can also cause people to misread you, so be careful not to make the wrong impression.

Your partner is quite possessive and your easy, extrovert disposition could cause misunderstandings and jealousy. Aside from that, your relationship has a better than average chance of being fulfilling for both of you and lasting a lifetime.

Your partner is a 2

You are creative, inspiring, optimistic, but also moody and sometimes cynical. Overall, you are easygoing and easy to get along with. You have a great sense of humor, you are outgoing, and you are a bit of a social butterfly. Your partner is intuitive, sensitive, gentle, and tactful, and made of quite a different cloth, yet the combination has a better-than-average chance of lasting a lifetime. But there is a caveat: you must watch what you say and how you say it.

You speak your mind, and you can be a little tactless at times, without realizing the effect your words have on your partner. Your partner is attracted to your impulsive, genuine, and often uninhibited behavior, but they are also extremely sensitive and quite capable of reading between the lines. It is easy for you to hurt them, and you may not even know you are doing it. Your partner, on the other hand, can be a little dramatic and may let emotions get the upper hand. You tend to be less affected by criticism or an emotional exchange, but your partner has less control of their emotions.

You should be conscious of this, because while your partner may seem vulnerable, they are also stronger than they appear, and if they are not happy, they will leave and never look back. Your partner, dramatic as they can be, is also very resilient and a true survivor. You would do well to pay close attention to their mood swings—recognize what causes them and give them your full attention. Don't hesitate to apologize, even if you don't really feel you are to blame. It is a small token of your love, and they will recognize it as such and appreciate it.

Your partner has a mysterious side, almost unreachable, yet always there. People with a 2 Life Path have an inborn antenna that picks up vibrations most other people miss. And while they are easily tempted to use a white lie when it suits them, you would be ill-advised to try it with them—they will pick up on it.

You have a wild streak and can be a bit irresponsible or impulsive. You get bored easily and are not always good at following through. You tend to drop projects halfway when you get excited about something else. You should work on discipline and stay the course because your partner needs to see stability. Your partner may have initially been attracted in part by your happy-go-lucky, playful, jovial attitude and your sense of humor, but in the long run they need to see that you can be serious and overcome distractions or even boredom to follow up on something you started if it's important enough.

On a more positive note, the combination of 3 and 2 is passionate and strong, and they complement each other in many areas. You travel well together and can be an impressive team in social settings—chances are quite a few people may experience a little envy when they see you together. You both are creative, and if you share a home, that will be obvious. Your partner has excellent taste, while you can create unusual and original art.

Your partner is a reliable source of support and has the kind of intuitive wisdom you may want to pay attention to; you can learn to accept and sense the invisible world from them, and they can learn to be less inhibited and more open to you.

Your partner is a 3

You both have the creative, happy-go-lucky 3 Life Path, which indicates you carry on lively conversations and inspire and motivate each other. You joke easily and appreciate each other's humor. You enjoy each other's company and comfortably share an active social life.

On the surface, there is little negative to say about this combination. However, a deeper look suggests that this happy-go-lucky nature of your relationship could become the root of persistent problems, unless you consistently work on finding a deeper emotional and spiritual bond. Both of you tend to gloss over rough spots when they emerge rather than dealing with them head-on. It is important that you address relationship issues as they arise; otherwise, they will fester and create bigger problems in the future.

Watch for subtle signs indicating something might be bothering your partner because, although you are both excellent communicators, you do not always use this talent to express your deeper, private feelings. Stay attentive. If you suspect something is up, even though your partner is doing what they can to hide it behind a jovial facade, sit down and have a frank and intimate talk about what is going on. You will have to consciously work on this, as neither one of you is naturally inclined to dig below the surface, especially when emotions are involved.

Another potential issue for this combination is that fun can become too high a priority, overshadowing important responsibilities and duties. The 3 Life Path tends to be scattered, unfocused, and impulsive—common traits in creative people and in the creative process. The 3 lets the mind wander in search of new, creative ideas. However, without effort and discipline, your creative ideas have little chance of materializing. You may need to remind each other to stay focused and keep your eyes on the goal.

Finally, you should be aware that a stable financial foundation and paying attention to the responsibilities of daily life, such as tracking expenses and preparing tax documents, are needed to live the kind of creative, sometimes impulsive lifestyle you both aspire to. For that reason, you may want to sit down and create a rule book or a schedule of duties you can share and help each other to be consistent in your chores. The fact is that most people with a 3 Life Path need help in those areas and do not do well when finances are difficult. You simply don't have the confidence and faith to carry you through those times. Your best defense is a good offense, and in this case, that means purposely working on preventing those problems from disrupting your otherwise happy lives.

All in all, while most people with identical Life Paths tend not to become romantically involved, the 3 is the exception. Your relationship has above-average potential of happiness and longevity.

Your partner is a 4

You are opposites in many ways, which makes this a promising albeit challenging combination. You are optimistic, creative, playful, unconventional, and easygoing. Your partner is more serious, grounded, pragmatic, and disciplined. Your partner has determination; once they set a goal, they will do whatever it takes to make it happen. You tend to go with the flow and are more likely to drop a goal if it appears out of reach or requires more effort and discipline than you are willing to give.

Your partner understands that control, focus, responsibility, and duty are required for a life of comfort and contentment and therefore takes it seriously, while you bring in a sunnier disposition and can lighten the atmosphere with a joke and a smile. This creates a balanced relationship if the going is easy. When times are difficult, these contrasting personalities can cause discord quickly and with devastating results. When challenges arise, especially financial ones, the 3 and 4 combination is at a disadvantage.

It is important for you both to recognize and accept the differences in your personalities and general view of your circumstances. This may not be easy because you are both likely to question how your partner could respond so differently to what you believe is the correct and required approach. You may feel that the effort your partner is making is unnecessary or misdirected, perhaps even detrimental to a positive outcome. Your partner may blame you for not making more of an effort, which may well be justified.

Try to understand that your partner needs to take practical steps; they need to feel they have some control over the situation. Although it may look like you are ignoring a problem or downplaying it to avoid taking responsibility, your partner should accept that your easygoing, optimistic nature allows you to take more time before jumping into action. You are not lazy; you simply feel that most problems resolve themselves if you just give it time.

Although your sharply differing perspectives could make things difficult at times, yours is a very promising combination. The key to making it the best relationship it can be lies in combining your individual qualities and not judging one another.

Your partner is a 5

This is an excellent combination, but because the partners are so compatible, they sometimes also enhance each other's less desirable traits.

You are upbeat, expressive, creative, and lighthearted, but you do not always maintain focus, nor are you particularly practical. Your partner is dynamic, social, and adventurous, with a tendency to overindulge. If you share a home, you will have little trouble creating a living environment and a lifestyle suitable for both of you.

You both communicate well, and your verbal skills make you a popular couple. In fact, one of the things that could trip you up is your social nature. Either of you could become jealous. You both thrive on taking center stage and enjoy the spotlight; this has the potential to create a competitive atmosphere.

Your partner will tend to say impulsive things that are hurtful or might allude to a personality issue you were unaware of. However, you will need to read between the lines, because your partner may not address it directly but rather cloud it with subtle statements.

A similar issue could arise from your inclination to skim over deeper issues, especially those that are emotional. Your partner should be aware that, even after years together, you may not easily reveal your deeper feelings. If you are not observant, either of you could be experiencing inner turmoil without the other being aware of it.

Generally, the 3 Life Path and the 5 Life Path get along very well. You are drawn to your partner's dynamic, exciting personality; your partner enjoys your wacky sense of humor and upbeat nature. This is a good combination that can last a lifetime.

If problems arise that jeopardize the relationship, it will likely be due to the lack of deep, personal communication. Both the 3 and 5 tend to stay somewhat on the surface and like to keep emotional issues on the back burner instead of dealing with them directly. But when the turbulence eventually reaches the surface, it is often too late to heal the discord that has festered.

It is essential that you confide in each other and pay close attention. Watch for subtle signs of unease or anger and deal with it immediately in an open, direct, and compassionate way. This is the key to sharing an inspiring, creative, happy life.

Your partner is a 6

You are a popular and creative couple. You have the verbal energy and sense of humor everyone enjoys, while your partner emanates the warmth and self-sacrificing love that easily wins the hearts of family and friends. You easily maintain a vibrant social life and a large circle of friends.

Your partner is a 6, nicknamed the father/motherhood number, and has the natural ability to draw loyalty and devotion from others that often lasts a lifetime. Healing and comforting are second nature to them, and they will do it unconditionally and indiscriminately.

You are a 3, also a giving and popular number—more playful and verbally creative than the 6, but less grounded and disciplined. Your energy is more impulsive. Unlike your partner, you probably don't have much patience for emotional issues. You can be a great shoulder for people to cry on if it doesn't take more than two minutes, in part due to your optimistic and lighthearted nature, which leads you to expect the same resilient and confident response to troubles and hardships from others. This can seem superficial and less responsive to your partner's need to share things on a deeper level, which in turn can become a cause of stress and resentment. It is therefore important that you listen to your partner and take their issues seriously.

Both of you will need to accept your differing perspectives and the approaches you take to sensitive matters. You should recognize that your partner is more easily affected by matters of the heart than you think is sensible. And your partner should understand that your cheery demeanor does not mean you are not fully committed to their well-being. Your partner needs to recognize that there is more to you than meets the eye, and you can help with that by giving your emotions the space and attention they need, instead of hiding them behind a cheerful facade.

The fact that, in general, you and your partner experience emotional turbulence so differently is not due just to your tendency to skim over these moments, but also because your partner tends to worry not only about their own circumstances but those of others. They tend to carry the burdens of the people around them; they want to be everything for everybody. This can irritate you because you sense that people sometimes take advantage of that.

Do your best to be sensitive to the emotional needs of your partner, while your partner should accept that you are made of a different cloth and need light and space to allow your creativity to express itself. You are not made to worry about others, or even yourself. You are the upbeat, inspiring, high-spirited person that can uplift others without even realizing you are doing it.

Your partner is a 7

The different natures of the 3 and 7 can make a relationship last for two weeks or a lifetime. If your relationship is stable and has existed for quite some time, you may well remain soulmates for life. If the relationship began recently and has already experienced some turmoil, you might be in for a rough ride. It is also quite common for this combination to turn from romance into a deep friendship soon after a romantic falling-out.

You have a restless, energetic, unconventional mind that happily explores the boundaries of creativity and originality. Like a kaleidoscope, the mind of the 3 easily changes color and shape and enchants those around it. However, the 3 also prefers to stay on the surface, keeping things light and upbeat.

Your partner has a more serious but no less unconventional way of viewing life. Your partner is a relentless seeker of truth and understanding who finds satisfaction in quiet moments of contemplation and soul-searching.

Although you have very different intellectual styles, you are both unconventional and not afraid to wander off the beaten path. You also differ in your needs and interests—but they are not incompatible per se. In fact, it is precisely your uniquely different intellects that make this relationship lively and interesting—or turbulent and short-lived.

To use an analogy, the 3 is like the sparkling, excited, playful child, and the 7 is the wise, more serious teacher. You complement each other and lend each other something you are not able to give yourselves. You bring an upbeat attitude and an intuitive, easygoing faith in life, while your partner offers a taste of the beauty found in exploring the deeper aspects of life itself. Like the sun and the moon, each in their different way, you supply light, energy, and comfort. If you can accept your differences, you should be able to live in harmony and find joy and fulfillment in this relationship.

Your partner is an 8

The 3 and the 8 carry very different traits, which are compatible in some areas but not in others. You have a creative, inspiring, uplifting, and somewhat scattered energy. Your partner is more ambitious, goal-oriented, and focused. Although you take differing approaches, you are both energetic and capable of turning dreams into reality—you just go about it in entirely different ways. This is not an easy combination for romance and long-term relationship commitment. However, this combination is often more successful between business partners or longtime friends. In a business environment, you would be the creative source while your partner would be the visionary.

Together, you could do very well. You are both good communicators. You can clarify an issue with a sense of humor and pinpoint precision, and your partner has a more practical approach by taking bold, decisive action. Therefore, you complement each other in many ways and are quite compatible. Unfortunately, when it comes to romance, the compatibility is less harmonious.

Your partner is ambitious, practical, dedicated to accomplishing their goals, and capable of sustained effort for a long period of time. You also have the energy and drive needed to make things happen but tend to drop a project when it is no longer interesting or when another project seems more important. You don't have your partner's sense of organization and focus, and you scatter your energies. This could irritate your partner, who feels that anything less than total commitment to a set goal is unacceptable.

You, on the other hand, will sometimes feel that your partner's priorities are too materialistic and usually connected to their own needs and expectations. You are more idealistic and easygoing.

Your partner believes in setting a goal and overcoming any obstacles and doing whatever it takes to reach that goal. You don't have that inflexible commitment and determination and are therefore comfortable dropping one project and trying something new.

Often, the 3 and the 8 get along quite well on the surface, but both of you must show a fair amount of tolerance and acceptance of your differences. The bottom line is that this relationship comes down to mutual respect and tolerance. Your relationship also has a better chance of happiness and longevity if you give each other plenty of space—perhaps even living separate but parallel lives.

Your partner is a 9

The 3 and the 9 have the potential to form a strong bond, one that lasts for a long time—if not forever. They represent archetypes that are almost mythical in their romantic alliance. Many stories of patience and self-sacrifice could be told about this union. What makes this so surprising is the fact that your compatibility is possible even though both numbers are considered self-centered, even egocentric at times.

You are both creative and have powerful imaginations and intense inner lives, but there are distinct differences in how you express them.

You have a unique, somewhat offbeat originality. You have faith that life will always be there for you and you don't sweat the little things. You take whatever comes your way in stride. Your inborn sense of hope and optimism make you attractive and is the reason you caught your partner's eye to begin with.

Your partner is more distant, not only in their personal relationships with friends, family, coworkers, or even you, but also in their outlook on life and the way they express their creativity. They stand back to widen their perspective, then use their vision to manipulate the environment until everything is harmonious. Your partner has the talent to combine colors and materials to create beauty in a disciplined manner. You admire the way your partner seems to control events and surroundings, and your partner appreciates the easy way you come up with original ideas and your impressive ability to verbalize your thoughts and your sense of humor. All of this brings balance to your relationship.

However, that same difference, your uninhibited, easy way of expressing your feelings and thoughts, and your partner's tendency to be somewhat aloof at times, can cause discord. You may become frustrated with your partner's lack of participation, while your partner may feel that you are superficial and even irresponsible. It is at that time that you and your partner need to consciously decide to sit down and talk about what bothers you, and it is in large part up to you to initiate the conversation because your partner will tend to withdraw and act as if nothing is wrong.

Another potential area of conflict can arise during social events. You love attention and can be the light of the party. Your sense of humor and easygoing manners can draw a crowd, and when that is the case, your partner, who is not as comfortable in the limelight as you are, may feel insecure and can even feel resentful. It is important that you pay attention to your partner so they don't feel left out.

Fortunately, the qualities you share outweigh the areas where you might clash. When a 3 Life Path and a 9 Life Path become romantically involved, there is an above-average possibility of a long and joyful relationship.

CHAPTER 4

Life Path 4

Your partner is a 1

Your initial attraction to your partner was at least in part due to their adventurous, devil-may-care courage and self-confidence, and their apparent ability to take in stride whatever comes their way. The 1 Life Path is a dynamic force, and that makes them attractive, especially to a more grounded and pragmatic person like you.

You like to know where the path you are on is going, whether it is your career or your relationship. Even your spiritual outlook on life thrives on logic and sensibility. You are the rock others rely on. You are trustworthy, dependable, and tend to keep your promises. You set your goals, plot the path that will get you there, and go for it.

Setting goals and the determination to reach them is what you have in common with your partner, but that is where the similarity ends. Your partner's approach is different; they don't plot the path, they just fire up their engines and go. This can be frustrating to you, especially if it is a shared goal, like saving for a house or building a business. It is interesting to note that a 4 and a 1 can be excellent business partners who complement each other very well, if there is no romantic relationship involved. When there is, things can become too personal for both of you, and instead of complementing, you may limit and frustrate each other.

It may seem illogical, but your chances of a long and harmonious relationship increase dramatically if you keep some distance and let your partner go about their life without trying to be constantly involved, and vice versa. Your partner's energy is not particularly subtle or carefully managed, and that can be harmful to you, as you tend to be a careful planner—turbulence of any kind bothers you, while your partner thrives on it. Your energy is controlled and is applied with care and an eye for detail, which, in your partner's eyes, can seem boring—your partner is more an adventurer and appreciates a more energetic, if not impulsive, approach. They see it as an opportunity to speed things up; it suits their dynamic energy.

The key to a long and happy relationship for you and your partner is to walk separate but parallel paths; do not try too hard to merge, because that is likely to cause friction. Your bond can be equally strong without the need to be absorbed in each other's lives.

You are the rock your partner can and will lean on. You bring stability, while your partner brings action and adventure. You need each other, but you don't need to be each other.

Your partner is a 2

Your romantic partner has all the qualities you appreciate in another person but feel might be lacking in you, and that is a major part of the attraction. The gentleness, the warmth, the intuition, the easy way they move in a social setting and make friends anywhere they go. You sometimes feel they live in a different reality—one where communication happens on many levels, not just words, and you are aware you are missing some of it. Your partner is skilled when it comes to making others feel comfortable and loved. They are everyone's friends, until they are not. Your partner is strongly influenced by feelings, and when those feelings are hurt, they can turn quite vicious.

You, on the other hand, are thoroughly grounded, rock-solid, and sensible. You are more a doer than a dreamer. You set goals and work toward them, steadily, single-mindedly, and with determination. You are eagle-eyed when it comes to details, and an excellent observer, but where you see the visible, material world clearly, your partner is more perceptive to a hidden world, to the subtle indicators that escape others, the body language, facial expressions, unspoken words—your partner is highly intuitive.

Your relationship has a strong foundation; you complement each other well and you can plan and build and work together. The practical, physical reality does not challenge your relationship often; you agree easily, and if you do not, your partner is generally the one to bend and let you have your way. However, it is the world of feelings where you may clash. You have some rough edges and have difficulty sensing the emotional impact words can have. You can absorb a fair amount of criticism or any verbal assault without being particularly affected, but your partner is much more vulnerable and easily hurt. Your partner can also get frustrated and annoyed when they sense what they perceive as a lack of emotional involvement; you can seem unaffected, even distant, but that is simply self-defense; you are not good at handling emotions—your own or those of others. Fortunately, this is an occasional issue and thanks to your partner's tact and diplomacy, it usually peters out and leaves you both unscathed.

Even as parents, you complement each other well; you are the steady, grounded influence, while your partner has the softer, gentler touch.

This is a promising relationship with an above-average chance of lasting love, respect, and a joyful life.

Your partner is a 3

This is a promising as well as an exceedingly difficult combination. Your partner has an optimistic, creative, playful, perhaps even childlike nature. They have faith in life, confident that everything will work out in the end. They are born optimists and have a natural and intuitive ability to go with the flow and avoid pitfalls almost effortlessly.

You, on the other hand, are more grounded and practical, with a hands-on approach to life. You feel that discipline, focus, responsibility, and duty are required for a life of comfort and contentment.

On one hand, these traits create a nicely balanced relationship. But when problems arise (such as financial concerns, loss of employment, or a costly illness) you will approach them methodically and with determination; you are not the type of person to sit back and watch things fall apart. Your partner tends to be confident and perhaps takes a "let's wait and see" approach. This may cause you to question their will and commitment toward sharing responsibility and effort to overcome the problem. That kind of blame can feed resentment and anger, which can turn you against each other and keep you from acting together to overcome obstacles. It is also somewhat misplaced, because while they may be slower in acting, their faith and positive outlook are a great source of comfort and strength and can motivate both of you when you are just about to give up.

You should recognize that you and your partner have very different personalities, and if your environment and circumstances are harmonious, you complement each other well and there is little or no stress or disagreement. In fact, to those around you, your relationship seems almost picture-perfect. It is in times of trouble that your different approaches can cause issues. It is important that you recognize that your partner's lighthearted attitude does not reflect a lack of care or concern but rather a deep-down determination that one way or another, they will fix whatever needs fixing.

You have reason to be grateful to be romantically involved with a person with a 3 Life Path, because you can be sure they will bring light and joy into your life. By the same token, they can, and almost certainly will, appreciate your hands-on, pragmatic approach to the day-to-day job of creating a nice and comfortable lifestyle.

Your partner is a 4

You both have a 4 Life Path, indicating a relationship that is either very compatible or extremely stressful—there is not much room in the middle. Your lifestyle preferences are likely very similar, and you both prefer a certain amount of predictability and routine in your lives. This does not mean you don't enjoy a surprise on occasion, but you generally want your daily routine to be firmly established and uninterrupted.

The success of your relationship relies largely on how compatible your daily routines are. Details are critical because you both tend to become irritated when your carefully established schedules are disturbed. It is important that you respect each other's needs and habits. You probably tend to create environments that are finely tuned and designed to accommodate your daily physical, mental, and spiritual needs.

Unless your habits are compatible, it will be difficult for you to sustain this relationship without making a few adjustments—aside from the necessary give-and-take of any relationship. Neither of you should severely limit your needs or desires to accommodate the other, as it will only work in the short term; try to arrange a somewhat separate routine instead. It is better to give each other room than to force things that are uncomfortable, creating minor annoyances that can turn into growing sources of resentment.

You are both reliable, dependable people who honor your promises. Being able to count on each other is a powerful ally in your relationship. However, if taken too far, your grounded, practical nature can also create a rigid lifestyle that could lead to frustration and gradual alienation from friends and family members. Lacking tolerance and acceptance of other people's lifestyles can put a stranglehold on your social life and, indirectly, a strain on your relationship.

Your key words for a successful, rewarding relationship are *tolerance* and *flexibility*.

Your partner is a 5

Yours is a challenging combination. You like routine and predictability, while your partner prefers change and the unexpected. The 4 and 5 are opposites in many ways. Interestingly, this is often the root of the initial attraction. You are drawn to your partner's daring, adventurous, energetic life. Your partner admires the control and discipline you display.

This combination often creates a dynamic relationship—not unlike a roller-coaster ride. Due to these extreme differences, your relationship will require mutual love and acceptance that is strong enough to weather your differing likes and dislikes, including your lifestyle preferences. Trying to change your partner is futile—your needs and desires are simply too different. You must accept the fact that your partner is not predictable and will never be happy living a highly structured life. Your partner needs to make peace with your need for an organized and controlled environment.

You will notice differences in other areas as well. Your partner is sensual and feels comfortable around others. They are social and have an adventurous side, even a wild streak. You, on the other hand, can be sociable but prefer to keep a certain amount of distance. When choosing companionship, you are more discriminating and tend to hold on to protocol longer. As a rule, you are more conventional and careful, whereas your partner can reveal an extroverted, even outrageous side given the right occasion.

When it comes to opinions, you often find yourselves on opposing sides. You need a structured connection to life, even in spiritual matters. Your partner's inner world is more imaginative and changeable. You may be willing to accept rules and regulations that your partner enjoys breaking. These examples should not be taken too literally; you are complex individuals with additional influences in other areas that could modify these aspects. Suffice it to say you will encounter differences in your personalities and your approaches to many issues.

Interestingly, this combination can be powerful, exciting, and long-lasting. The key to success will be in not taking yourself or your concepts too seriously—something you may need to work on. Maintain a sense of humor and keep in mind that opinions are just that and have relative values. Focus on enjoying each other's company; combine your strengths and build on your differences.

Your polarity has the potential to create a dynamic, rewarding relationship. With tolerance and openness, you can build a healthy relationship where your partner's dynamic, adventurous spirit and your disciplined and methodical approach happily live side by side.

Your partner is a 6

It is uncommon for these two numbers to become romantically involved. Although they carry common traits—they are both practical and highly responsible—they are rarely interested in each other. The 4 Life Path and the 6 Life Path are both family-oriented numbers, with a strong sense of community and loyalty to others, but they tend to compete where you might expect them to be supportive.

However, if support prevails over competition and you become involved in a romantic relationship, it will usually be a strong, comfortable alliance—the kind of relationship others view as indestructible. If you can accept your differences, you have the potential to be the "perfect couple."

You share important priorities: your home, children, friends, stability, and security. You are both loyal and protective of each other and those you care about. It is in your approach to life and the way you express yourselves that you are quite different.

While you rely on structure, discipline, and control to protect and care for others, your partner relies on warmth, sacrifice, and forgiveness. You are less flexible and may, at times, feel that your partner is too soft and lenient. Yours is an example of a relationship typically characterized by the disciplinary parent versus the one who views parenting as simply showering their children with love and letting them be.

People around you may have the impression that you are rigid and less loving, while your partner is pure love and gentleness; however, this is not an accurate characterization. Your love is no less powerful than your partner's—it is just less openly expressed. You will fight for them and sacrifice just about anything to protect your partner, your children, and anyone who is part of your life.

Some danger exists if your differing attributes become too magnified. Your need for discipline and structure could become too much for your partner, suffocating and limiting your partner's ability to express love naturally and without inhibition. Your partner's willingness to be generous to a fault—and possibly be taken advantage of as a result—might lead you to lose respect for them or think of them as weak and gullible—and that may not be entirely incorrect. However, your partner has a strong core and a powerful belief that love will conquer all, and therefore they can afford to appear soft. They know that when push comes to shove, they will prevail.

Ultimately, your relationship will last and give you what you need if you share your love—the love your partner expresses generously, while you offer it more reluctantly, but a love that is no less committed and powerful. Both of you are people who understand and appreciate commitment, and this helps you overcome friction because your commitment and love can outlast any discord.

Your partner is a 7

Your combination is almost made in heaven. "Almost" because you likely have a few sharp angles that need smoothing. Your numbers suggest this relationship is founded more on intellect and inner, spiritual connections than on the sensual, physical plane.

You are practical, grounded, and goal-oriented. You can take an idea, quickly determine whether it is doable, and bring it to fruition. You are of the earth. Your partner, on the other hand, is the seeker: philosophical, intellectual, a bit of a dreamer, and full of ideas. Earth (you) and sky (your partner—symbolically speaking) are in this together, and neither can exist without the other.

This combination is often found among relationships that started early in life—high school sweethearts perhaps. The numbers are drawn to each other because what each has to offer is exactly what the other needs. You are attracted to your partner's abstract and philosophical outlook on life. It inspires a sense of freedom and space that is less defined in your solid, dependable, but sometimes too structured and restrictive views.

You offer your partner a stable, secure port in an internal universe that is often chaotic and unstable. You understand the dangers that lurk in the corners of the subconscious when the mind wanders too far into the realm of dreams and abstract fears. Where you offer stability, peace, and comfort, your partner brings freedom to your more restrictive mental approach. The complementary traits of the 4 Life Path and the 7 Life Path create a romance that can last a lifetime.

The areas where you may need to compromise are of the more mundane, material type. While you require order and respectability and feel rather uncomfortable and insecure without it, your partner prefers a bit of chaos and is less concerned about the approval of others. If you are successful in accommodating each other in these areas, you should be able to get as close to being "soulmates" as any two people can.

Your partner is an 8

This is an excellent combination for romance as well as business. The 4 Life Path and the 8 Life Path have the potential to connect perfectly and enhance each other's power. By joining forces, they triple or quadruple their output—the sum becomes much more than the parts. This is considered the best blend of archetypes for a business partnership. You deliver the persistence, determination, dependability, and the detail-oriented, methodical approach necessary to reach your goal, while your partner brings the vision and conviction that the goal should be bigger, and that no dream is unattainable.

Fortunately, a similar synergy exists for romance as well. Although you are different in many ways, you respect and recognize each other's value. Together, you can create an environment of love, trust, and deep bonding.

You and your partner have the potential to become an almost perfect combination. However, dangers do exist as they do in any relationship, especially when it comes to recognizing whether something is realistic or not. You are the voice of caution, while your partner is perfectly willing to take a risk, even one that could, if the project fails, put you in a very difficult spot. Your partner will likely try something that you find outrageous and doomed to fail. Your partner's stubborn determination and at times authoritarian approach could become a major irritant to you.

When that happens, the best move is simply to disengage. Communicate your ideas, but don't try too hard to persuade your partner to give up a plan or a goal they believe in. Alternately, your partner may see you as a stick-in-the-mud who limits their potential and keeps a project from even getting off the ground. In this situation, your partner should recognize that this does not signify a lack of courage on your part but that you are not willing to take such a risk or waste your time on something you are convinced is not doable. In these situations, feelings of frustration could overshadow the love and respect that is the foundation of your relationship.

All partnerships must compromise, and this is true for your relationship as well. Your partner is very independent, and sharing feelings does not come naturally to them. Sometimes, they will disconnect because they need distance to express their independence. This makes you feel they are detached and maybe they don't care so much anymore. Your challenge is to not let insecurity and doubt get in the way and do exactly the opposite of what you would like to do: allow them space and freedom so they don't feel smothered, and you will find that after a while they are back, and the connection is as strong as it ever was.

It is not unheard of for this combination to survive several major breakups and reconciliations, even divorce and remarriage. After all, you have more in common than you might be aware of, and when you are apart, you will miss that connection, the recognition that you are a good fit; like the gears in an engine, you make each other stronger, faster, more capable. If those gears are properly tuned, the sky is the limit, both in your romance and in your worldly ventures.

Your partner is a 9

The fact that you and your partner are in a close relationship of any kind is both remarkable and promising.

Have you ever met someone you had an immediate dislike for, or perhaps just experienced an inability to relate to on almost any level? No two numbers generate that kind of inexplicable, uncomfortable vibration as clearly as your 4 and your partner's 9. Fortunately, if you are currently in a successful relationship and no longer in the early stages of exploring your feelings for someone, it's likely that a strong physical attraction helped you overcome the common but unwarranted feelings of antagonism.

Still, your Life Path numbers reveal important differences you will need to address to develop a satisfying, long-lasting relationship. Your challenges stem from the difficulty the 4 and 9 have of seeing eye to eye. The problem is not so much that they are incompatible; they simply don't easily relate to each other's viewpoints.

The success of your relationship lies in large part in your willingness to give each other a great deal of freedom. Think of this relationship as two strangers who love each other. Some relationships require deep, intimate sharing of ideas, even secrets and inner experiences. This would most likely not only be uncomfortable for you, but it may not be possible. You carry very different attitudes and approaches to life. Oddly, in your relationship, the motto should probably be "the less I know, the better." The less you try to "understand" your partner, the more you will be able to allow love to meld your hearts. Openness, acceptance, and respect are key.

You must accept your partner's need to devote time and attention to people and projects you do not relate to or are not passionate about, and your partner will need to compromise as well. As idealistic as your partner is, a 9 can be self-righteous and annoyingly opinionated—and likely irritated by your pragmatic nature—so it's a classic example of the idealist versus the realist. You will never change your partner. Even with the best intentions, asking them to see things from your perspective will be counterproductive and often create more distance, confusion, and alienation.

There is hope, however, and the potential for a successful, loving relationship if you can accept the fact that you will frequently take different paths. Understand there will most likely always be some distance between you. But if there is, remember that a little separation is the only thing that makes it possible for you to live in harmony. Eliminate the distance, and the harmony could easily be disrupted.

CHAPTER 5

Life Path 5

Your partner is a 1

These are some of the more compatible numbers, and you can be assured there will rarely be boredom or complacency in such a dynamic and passionate relationship. However, it is not without peril, as that same dynamic energy can also quickly turn turbulent, if not explosive. Yours is a relationship that feels alive and always intense, in large part because, subconsciously, you are also aware of the ever-present danger. The sense that anything can happen at any time is a major ingredient in your relationship, and it suits both of you well.

On the upside, you complement each other and share several similar traits. You are both risk takers, willing to try something new or adapt to changing circumstance, albeit in your case, your ability to accept the unexpected and adapt quickly is in large part due to your energetic, somewhat undisciplined energy; you are all about freedom and going places, you have a relatively short attention span, you abhor routine, and there is nothing predictable about you.

Your partner is equally suited to a vibrant lifestyle, but with a different spin. Your partner is more goal-oriented and, while quite capable of accepting changes as they come, they will continue to aim for their goal. Your partner can be extremely persistent and is unlikely to give up. You, on the other hand, are rather quick to drop one goal in exchange for another. You are more impulsive and less likely to stay the course. You are driven by enthusiasm, but when that diminishes, so does your focus. This can cause some frustration for your partner, who feels that perhaps you are giving up too quickly.

For this relationship to grow and last, you will need to work on self-discipline, not only in setting and reaching goals, but also in your life-style choices. You have a wild streak, and while, to your partner, that is an important part of your attraction, when they feel you are no longer in control, their attraction will turn into disappointment, and that is something you want to avoid. Your partner has a powerful sense of pride, and seeing you diminished as a person will greatly harm the relationship. Your partner wants to idolize you, to feel their self-worth is enhanced by your love and your presence, because otherwise, they will themselves feel diminished, and for a 1, that is not an option.

If you maintain the effort and self-control to earn your partner's devotion, this will be a wonderful relationship capable of withstanding any outside influence that might harm it. Your partner is by nature loyal and extremely protective, but also hardheaded and somewhat judgmental. You are more open-minded and you easily accept, or even adopt, a different point of view.

Your partner may be flexible when it comes to changing circumstances, but that flexibility does not apply to their beliefs or opinions. This can become a source of arguments and, with a relationship that exists so close to the edge, that can easily escalate into something quite destructive. It will be up to you to be patient, to allow room to breathe, to back down—not because you are weak, but because you need to understand that for your partner to change their ideas, they need time and they need to feel that change comes from them, not from you or anyone else. They are stubborn, so just give them space.

Discipline and moderation from you, and mental and spiritual flexibility from your partner, are the keys to making this a happy and lasting relationship. It may never feel particularly stable, but it will feel vibrant, alive, intense, and passionate.

Your partner is a 2

You are dynamic and adventurous, and you thrive on change. Your flexible, unconventional, and nonconformist outlook on life is ruled largely by the mind; you have a powerful imagination, you dream large and aim high, but you do not always have the staying power to see your endeavors through to completion. You are restless and all too willing to drop a project when the going gets tough.

Your partner is different; they want stability and prefer a predictable and reliable partner. For your partner, feelings rule, and the human connection is all-important. Your partner is emotional and vulnerable, but also persistent and capable of getting others to work together and make great things happen.

The 5 Life Path and 2 Life Path do not easily form friendships and are generally better suited for business partnerships, but if romance does come into the picture, they are proverbial examples of love at first sight. Your relationship is intensely passionate and sensual and probably felt that way from the moment you met. However, you express your love quite differently. You thrive on a physical touch, and you are a wonderful partner. You are generous with expressing your love in all the possible ways, except emotional—not because you don't feel it but because you do not trust yourself to express it properly. You touch and speak of love, and it is sincere and genuine, but you tend to maintain an emotional distance, and your partner is the exact opposite—to them, it's about feelings.

Your partner is extremely sensitive and has an innate understanding of what the other person needs. You are better on the physical plane—not because you are superficial, but because for you, love is felt and shared by the power of touch. Your heart sings when you feel your partner's love in their touch. Your partner's heart is touched by emotional expressions of love.

For that reason, a lasting, long-term, and harmonious relationship is possible only if you accept each other as you are. Your partner should know that while you may not always express your feelings the way they do, the feelings are there, and they are real.

As mentioned before, the 2 and 5 can be excellent business partners as well, because when feelings are not part of the relationship, you do quite well. And that, perhaps, best illustrates the challenging side of your relationship: you do better when you stay on the surface. When the heart is involved, you don't match as well as you, and especially your partner, might want to.

You are both good communicators. Use that to try and understand each other. Be tolerant of your differences and generous in your loving, and this relationship may well last a lifetime.

Your partner is a 3

This is a highly compatible combination, not only because you have a lot in common, but also because the areas in which you differ complement each other well.

You are spontaneous, freedom-loving, and a bit of an adventurer. Your partner is creative, witty, and generally upbeat. You both have good verbal skills and tend to be the life of the party in social settings. You are most likely a popular couple; however, this can also create a competitive atmosphere and become a cause of stress and envy. It is important that you give your partner their time in the limelight and try not to interrupt or one-up them in social situations.

Problems can arise that jeopardize this relationship if neither of you makes the effort to have deeper, more emotionally or spiritually involved conversations. You both tend to skim the surface and keep such issues on the back burner instead of dealing with them directly. However, if issues or feelings are not handled decisively, they can fester and turn ugly, and eventually bubble up to the surface, causing discord. Fortunately, your partner can keep things lighthearted and playful even under those circumstances, and while that may also be somewhat superficial, it helps to find common ground and understanding without causing too much damage and drama.

You should also be aware that your partner needs an organized and stable environment because they tend to be highly creative but also unfocused and undisciplined in their approach to projects or goals. They benefit greatly from a guiding and supportive partner, and that too is a challenge because you have a dynamic, restless nature and are not particularly concerned about stability or predictability in your life. In fact, you love your freedom, and this is another reason being romantically involved with a 3 Life Path suits you well, because your partner is not likely to interfere with your freedoms—they are by nature tolerant and believe in live and let live.

The promise and potential of your relationship lies not in the usual recipe of dependence, commitment, and involvement with each other, but in the creative, playful nature of your partner, which pairs well with your energetic, curious mind that is always looking for something new. Nothing is more harmful to your desire to be with someone than boredom, and that is one thing you don't have to worry about in this relationship.

Your partner is a 4

This is not unlike a marriage between chaos and order. You love change and freedom, and you don't like to be tied down. Your partner is the opposite; they prefer order and predictability. They are dependable, reliable, trustworthy, and perhaps, in your eyes, sometimes a bit of a stick-in-the-mud. You are flexible, adaptable, capable of changing on a dime, and at times can be a little irresponsible.

You are loyal to a fault, but it is not easy for you to commit yourself and stick with it. You have a dynamic, restless nature and you need to know that you can change your lifestyle or your environment any time you want. Freedom is your most precious commodity.

Your partner, on the other hand, prefers a structured, predictable, even routine lifestyle, with as few changes as possible. They are perfectly capable of planning a path toward a different lifestyle, but it must be a realistic, step-by-step approach. It cannot be impulsive.

You are more spontaneous, not only in planning your future or changing your path, or even your career, but also in social situations; you are the extrovert, and your sense of humor is one of the things your partner loves, but they are also a little critical and maybe even envious of it.

It is not impossible for this relationship to be extremely satisfying and long-lasting, but it will take work. On your part, you need to accept your partner's need for stability and discipline. They are moderate and careful in the way they live. You must avoid trying to push them into situations they are uncomfortable with—that includes a lack of financial security and direction, and anything they consider unnecessarily risky.

On an intellectual and moral level, you will find there are many differences as well, and they are not always compatible. You tend to be more outrageous and unconventional in your opinions. You are highly sensual and more adventurous, while your partner tends to be more traditional and values established norms and rules. In many ways, this offers opportunities to both of you: you can influence your partner to be less inhibited, more easygoing, and less concerned with what others expect. Your partner can be a stabilizing influence and thereby help you reach your goals instead of surrendering to your tendency to quit when the going gets tough or when you simply lose interest. Your partner is good at pushing themselves and others to greater heights and admirable performances; they are good motivators by example.

The most valuable qualities you and your partner need to make the relationship work are respect and tolerance. If you try to change your partner to be more like you, it will not work and almost certainly will ruin the relationship. The same applies to your partner; you cannot, should not, and will not change to fit another mold, and any attempt to control you or to minimize your freedom will fail spectacularly.

Give each other space. Live together yet separate, but share your thoughts and feelings, and your relationship has an excellent chance of happiness and longevity.

Your partner is a 5

You and your partner both have a 5 Life Path, a number full of contradictions no matter where it is found. For example, the 5 is sensual, freedom-loving, tends to overindulge, and does not like to be tied down.

Paradoxically, you are loyal and less likely to cheat than any other number. The 5 will avoid commitment if possible but takes fidelity very seriously once they have committed. You probably recognize these traits in yourself and your partner. You are reluctant to tie yourself down, and even when you are committed, you are willing to give each other space and freedom. You are tolerant, easygoing, and flexible, and you will likely have an exciting, dynamic, and sensual connection. Both of you like exploring new places, trying new things, and living life to the fullest. Your mutual understanding and sharing of these traits is one of the many strong benefits to this combination that will help you weather many storms. However, there is a dangerous side to this relationship as well.

The danger does not come from outside, but from inside. You are both adventurous people who dislike routine, preferring change and variety in your lifestyle and environment. You adapt easily, even to major changes such as switching careers or moving to another town. You thrive on freedom and, to some extent, even chaos. This attraction to freedom and adventure has the potential to create trouble. Your desire to try new things and to test boundaries might be expressed in a somewhat wild lifestyle that includes overindulgence in drugs, alcohol, or other unhealthy or dangerous pastimes.

In most partnerships, if one partner has a "wild streak," the other can help to counter it. But in sharing the dynamic 5 energy, you could both venture into the danger zone with no one to prevent things from getting out of control.

You have much in common and have all the ingredients for a long, happy, and fun-filled relationship. However, to prevent a slow slide into a lifestyle that could be quite difficult to emerge from, you will both need to be painfully honest with yourselves and each other. If you see yourself or your partner moving toward an unhealthy habit, act swiftly to address it before it gets out of control. Have fun, but do not allow your desire for freedom and adventure to pull you too far in the wrong direction. The 5, more than any other number, requires discipline.

Your partner is a 6

The 5 and the 6 complement each other very well. You are attracted to your partner's strength and stability as the grounding force in your relationship, offering almost unconditional love and protection. Your partner makes you feel safe and secure because that is what the 6 thrives on: giving love, comfort, and protection.

Your partner, on the other hand, is attracted to your free spirit and the way your courage, adventurism, and curiosity brings excitement and joy to the relationship.

It is interesting to note that this type of partnership is rare, due to the initial distrust the 6 and the 5 must overcome when they first meet. They have very little in common and usually don't make the effort to bridge the gap. Therefore, love at first sight is seldom found in this combination, and when a 5 and 6 are drawn to each other, it is usually very physical and sensual. It is therefore likely that you had an instant and powerful physical attraction to your partner, which grew over time, gaining depth and a truer love, eventually overshadowing just about everything else in your lives. This physical attraction is a strong foundation, and while many couples tend to experience a decrease in their physical relationship as time goes by, your attraction will last and remain quite powerful. This is particularly important to you because you are an above-average sensual person by nature, whereas for your partner, the feeling of emotional and intellectual intimacy is the driving force.

Once your partner has overcome any initial wariness, which despite the initial attraction will be present, they will recognize that there is more depth and substance to you than they expected. It may take some time, but your partner will come to realize that the notion that people who value their freedom and love change, typical to those with a 5 Life Path, are reluctant to commit, is wrong.

In contrast, your partner could become a source of frustration or jealousy, because the 6 gives love freely and generously to all. Your partner is quick with hugs and concern for other people simply because they have a lot of love to give. Teaching, healing, and counseling, even if they are not part of your partner's career, are major ingredients in the makeup of a 6, and your partner needs avenues to express them.

The most difficult challenge your partner may have to overcome is your extremely social personality. You aspire to live a dynamic life full of change, impulsive decisions, social activities, freedom, and travel, while your partner thrives on stability and the sense of being part of a community of friends and family with whom they can interact daily. Your partner likes to feel needed, while you abhor that. This can become a source of friction. To maintain a successful relationship, the two of you will need to accept your differences while making a united effort to support and nourish your relationship.

Your partner is a 7

This is one of the best combinations for a long-lasting relationship and a merging of archetypes that promises intellectual and inner growth for both of you. The 5 Life Path and the 7 Life Path fulfill each other's needs and desires in many ways, but particularly on the mental and spiritual planes. Many famous intellectual and artistic couples share this combination. This partnership is larger and more promising than the sum of its parts.

You have a quick and flexible mind spiced with a wicked, offbeat sense of humor. Neurologists have suggested that over time, the mind begins to think according to repetitive patterns it develops, like water running through a canyon. This may be the case for many people, but not for you. A 5 Life Path will never allow their mind to shelter in repetitive, predictable patterns. Thanks to your ability to juggle ideas and concepts, you will seem younger and remain more playful and quick-witted long past the time others of your age have slowed down.

Your partner's mind is also powerful; however, their mental and spiritual faculties operate very differently from yours. Your partner has a dry sense of humor and a more serious mind. They seek answers to life's important questions and often spend time in contemplation searching for insight and understanding. It is likely your partner is not closely associated with an organized religion but nonetheless has a strong sense of the reality of the "God force." For them, the mystery of life is not an unattainable or abstract concept—it is a reality. The 7 is the most spiritual and intellectual of all numbers, but it is rarely found among those with traditional mindsets; the 7 asks too many questions and does not take anything at face value.

The only real source of discord that appears between the 5 and 7 is spiritual in nature. Your partner may feel your dynamic, social nature is too flamboyant or superficial at times. You might feel your partner becomes too invested in spiritual concepts or is unable to enjoy the simple pleasures of life; their serious approach can be a little frustrating to you. It may be difficult for you to understand how people can become so invested in abstract concepts and philosophies. And your partner may find it difficult to accept that you believe experiencing life is more important than analyzing it.

Fortunately, the 7 and the 5 have such a positive influence on each other that these differing outlooks rarely create problems. You keep your partner flexible and able to enjoy life from a simpler, more direct perspective, and your partner demonstrates how a deep, serious search for understanding can be immensely gratifying.

Your partner is an 8

You are adventurous and spontaneous; you enjoy exploring new experiences and ideas. You are quite sociable and enjoy meeting people. You likely have a natural talent for communication and persuasion. Your partner, on the other hand, tends to be driven by a desire for success and material wealth. Those with an 8 Life Path are natural leaders and often skilled at managing resources and taking calculated risks. They are determined and resilient and can overcome obstacles with relative ease. When the 5 and 8 come together in a romantic relationship, there can be a good balance of excitement and practicality.

However, there will also be some challenges to overcome. Your partner may at times see you as too flighty or inconsistent, which may clash with their more focused and disciplined nature. You may see your partner sometimes as too rigid or materialistic, which can be overwhelming and intimidating for your more free-spirited nature.

In the long run, your compatibility will be most harmonious and fulfilling for both of you if your roles in the relationship are different and somewhat separate. You both have unique qualities, but they rarely overlap. Perhaps the best way to describe the differences between your numbers is to look at them from a business perspective rather than a romantic one.

As business partners, you could do very well—if you play different roles. You would be excellent at promotion and sales. You are dynamic, articulate, and you think fast and often outside the box. You can see through people, which helps you influence others and resolve personality issues. You are likable and easygoing; most people are quite comfortable around you. Your partner is a visionary, has a strong commanding presence, and can be somewhat an authoritarian. Your partner would mostly be focused on a future goal. They are the executive, while you would be on the marketing side. These are very different qualities that can work well together if you recognize neither should try to tell the other how to do their job.

In a romantic relationship between the 5 and the 8, a similar picture emerges. If you are not tempted to tell your partner how to behave or what should be a priority, everything should be just fine. Another area of potential discontent can be on the physical plane. You tend to be quite sensuous and prefer someone who is generous in their expressions of love, be it verbal or physical. Your partner is less romantic and physical and may be hesitant to reach out and express their love. Their usual assertive approach does not apply to romance. They tend to be inhibited and they prefer that you take the initiative.

Finally, a word to the wise; your sociable and spontaneous nature may occasionally cause feelings of envy or jealousy in your partner. Be on guard to make sure they feel included.

Ultimately, the success of this relationship depends on how well both of you can appreciate and balance each other's strengths and weaknesses. Communication, compromise, and mutual respect are key factors in building a strong and harmonious partnership. It's important for both partners to find a balance between their desire for adventure and their need for stability and security.

Your partner is a 9

The fact that you are in a romantic relationship is somewhat surprising, and certainly uncommon. If you have been in a relationship with your partner for several years, you have overcome many potential obstacles, and probably will overcome anything in the future that comes your way. It is a clear indication that your relationship is strong and based on a powerful connection despite your many differences. A relationship between a 5 Life Path and a 9 Life Path is either very short-lived or has an excellent chance of lasting a lifetime. Either way, your likes and dislikes are quite different. You are sociable and outgoing. You carry your heart on your sleeve and know how to enjoy the many pleasures life offers. You try new things, you are an adventurer, you are outspoken, and you have, at times, a quick and sharp tongue. You inspire and motivate others, you are spontaneous and can turn on a dime. People are naturally drawn to you. Your partner is more subdued and deliberate in their approach to events and people—they don't like being in the limelight, unless it is to further an important cause. Your partner is idealistic and has a powerful sense of justice. They want to change the world for the better. They are less focused on the small community they live in—family, friends, neighbors, coworkers—than on people across the globe; they are the least prejudiced and are drawn to other cultures and continents. Your partner takes life's responsibilities seriously, while you tend to fly by the seat of your pants and rely on an inborn sense of faith that everything will be all right.

Where you see the world as a playground, they see it as their duty to work on it in one way or another, and as a result they may see you as superficial. One area you have in common is that you both love to travel, but again, for very different reasons. Your partner wants to bring positive change and dedicate time and effort to the betterment of mankind. You want to play and discover and challenge the unknown.

You are also more sensual and enjoy the many ways we can express our love for our partner, whereas your partner is less inclined to indulge in the simple pleasures we can experience, and this can be frustrating for you. Your partner can also seem distant and aloof at times, and you may feel you can't reach them. You should know that your partner is no less committed and feels as strongly as you do; they just don't like to display their affection except in privacy and special moments.

Although there is not much to be done about these differing outlooks, nor should you try to change them, the relationship between a 5 and a 9 is far from doomed. Other aspects of your personalities have the potential to be strongly connected and compatible, and if you have been in this relationship for several years, it means they outweigh your differences. You are both able to adapt to changes and you're willing to compromise, although there too you are more flexible than your partner—a trait you should take advantage of. In addition, neither of you was quick at committing to a relationship, since you both love space and freedom, you more than your partner. And while your desire for freedom is also based on entirely different needs—you because you hate routine and limitations of any kind, your partner because they want to be able to go anywhere they feel they are needed—you both understand this need and allow for it without letting petty feelings like jealousy and selfishness get in the way.

It is helpful if you know where to adjust or accept differences that strengthen your relationship. For your partner, it is important to recognize that idealism, self-righteousness, duty, and responsibility will impress you only if they don't take credit for their actions; you have an innate sense of distrust to excessive idealism and can't stand self-righteousness—something your partner may occasionally indulge in.

As for you, accept that your partner may often appear to live in a world of their own, may be hard to reach, and may not seem very interested in what is going on with you. Their commitment is strong, and you are not losing out on their love and attention. They just don't express it often, or easily.

Finally, you sometimes appear shallow or selfish in your partner's eyes, not because you are, but because your partner connects depth with idealism. Your energetic, adventurous, and spontaneous nature is rather foreign to them. You will need to compromise and be diplomatic when they call you on their perception that you lack depth, and not be insulted. Their love is strong and committed, and you may consider being involved in some of their lofty endeavors—it will greatly strengthen the relationship.

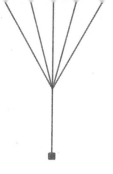

CHAPTER 6

Life Path 6

Your partner is a 1

You have chosen a partner who is vastly different from you, but still a good fit. In many ways, you complement each other.

You are loving and caring and you put family and friends before your own needs. You are self-sacrificing, and likely a bit gullible, especially with predators who know how to tug your heartstrings, so you have probably been taken advantage of.

Your partner is a leader, driven and ambitious, and will not allow anyone to take advantage of you. Your partner, if anything, may at times get annoyed with your willingness to help others, often in circumstances and for reasons they do not agree with. You like to be involved, you are a natural healer and teacher, and you display those qualities generously among those close to you. In the eyes of your partner, that's a recipe for disaster, as they are not nearly as trusting as you tend to be.

Your partner may at times seem selfish, especially next to you, as you are often selfless to a fault. It is important for you to remember that your partner is not devoid of empathy; they just have strict rules and expectations regarding qualities such as a strong work ethic, perseverance, and ambition in others, which they also demand of themselves. Your partner abhors weakness, while you are more forgiving and willing to help even those who, by your partner's rules, don't deserve it.

Your partner is loyal and protective of you but may push that too far and become controlling, even overbearing. Your natural inclination will be to surrender to that, in part owing to your aforementioned self-sacrificing nature, but also because your partner can be quite forceful. It is important that you not give in to that and instead be assertive and stand your ground. Not only to maintain a healthy relationship but also because your partner may lose respect and, in their eyes, that is unforgivable. Your partner values pride and self-confidence and if they perceive that to be lacking in their partner, it will damage the relationship.

Likewise, you may at times be bothered by your partner's apparent coldness and cruelty to others. But keep in mind that your partner, more than you, sees themselves as a buffer between the harsh reality of the world and the sanctity of their home and family; they are the warrior, the protector, and shielding those they love from harm is their priority. In that way, their coldness reflects their love, not the lack thereof.

Your partner is a 2

Your numbers are compatible and overlap in many ways. You are both emotionally accessible and aware; neither of you feels a need to hide your feelings. This is a major part of the potential for a passionate and lasting relationship. However, there are areas of your personality where you are quite different from your partner.

You are both strongly affected by the emotional, mental, or physical well-being of others; however, your partner is sensitive in ways most people are not; highly intuitive and capable of reading subtle signs in facial expression and body language, they are not easily fooled and it's difficult to hide your true feelings. It is therefore important that you be open, honest, and accessible.

At times, your partner's emotional sensitivity can become extreme and they can be melodramatic. They are vulnerable, and they know it, but it can also make them jealous and possessive. You would do well to keep in mind that while they may be easily hurt, they are not weak by anyone's measure. They bend, but they don't break; they are survivors, and anyone who finds themselves at the wrong end of their anger will likely be surprised by the power and intensity of their displeasure.

On the upside, their love is their life; they are passionate and committed, if the relationship is harmonious. When it isn't, you are in trouble. They will let you know, and they will not let you off the hook until you have apologized or changed your ways.

You are love personified, especially with family and friends and your community. You will sacrifice your own needs in favor of someone you care for. Seeing another in discomfort hurts you and you will jump into action to look for a way to fix it. These qualities make you popular, and there are likely quite a few people who have strong feelings of love and appreciation for who you are. And those same qualities are also a part of the reason your relationship has a good chance of lasting and bringing happiness to you both.

The most dangerous trait to your relationship is jealousy. Your partner will have to accept that there are quite a few others who thrive on your love and attention, and although this is often expressed in friendship (although there are likely some secret or not-so-secret admirers), your partner may have some difficulty recognizing and accepting that. So, keep your eyes open, and when you have even the slightest sense your partner may be feeling vulnerable, reach out and do what it takes to make them feel confident in your commitment.

Your partner is a 3

You are a giver, a healer, a guiding force. You are deeply involved, mentally and emotionally, with the well-being of others. Your heart is what guides you, and your empathy and compassion are front and center of who you are. Your friends and family are crucial to your happiness, but you worry about them more than you probably should. There are times when your attention to their needs makes them feel smothered. Your partner is quite different and not particularly compatible. However, you can learn from each other and enrich your life in ways few other number combinations can.

Your partner is upbeat and optimistic by nature. Like any other person, there can certainly be dark days, but their default state is one of confidence and joie de vivre. You both are creative, albeit in different ways—your creativity is more visual, while your partner's is verbal or leans toward performance art. Your partner is the kind of person who can entertain a crowd, and that's particularly obvious in social settings. They like the limelight, but they can also appear superficial and uncaring. However, that is only on the surface; your partner loves and cares deeply; they just don't like to dwell on what they perceive as depressing or melodramatic until the issue becomes too overwhelming. It is then that they show their loyalty and commitment in words and actions.

You are more responsible and organized than your partner, and this may cause resentment, but it isn't always your partner's chaotic and seemingly irresponsible lifestyle that causes you stress. You can be quite demanding and intolerant of perceived character weaknesses. It is better if you absorb some of their sunny disposition and are less concerned with order and discipline. Your partner understands deep down inside that life is to be enjoyed, and you would be better for it if you allowed yourself to soak up some of that.

The bottom line is that you are very different, and not always compatible, but you complement each other and can grow to become durable life partners. Your partner needs room and freedom and at least some chaos to let their needs and talents flow. Your challenge will be to be tolerant and accepting in order to make that happen.

Your partner is a 4

It is unlikely that you were instantly attracted to your partner—this was almost certainly not a case of love at first sight. However, the fact that you did become romantically involved means that you recognized qualities in your partner you really appreciate, such as their unwavering loyalty and dependability.

You are by nature warm and outgoing. You are not particularly chatty, nor are you someone who desires the limelight, but you tend to reach out and offer your love to anyone you encounter. Your partner is quite different. They are more reserved and distant. Your partner's strength and confidence are based on a solid core, a foundation of discipline and tenacity. They are less driven by feelings and more by a sense of responsibility and duty. You are all about feelings, and this difference is why a 6 and a 4 don't usually become a couple. But when they do, there is a lot of promise, and it can become a strong and lasting relationship.

While you have rather different personalities, you have similar priorities: family, the home, friends. You are both focused on the smaller community, the people close to you. A possible area of discontent can be that you are very trusting, perhaps at times even a little gullible, and your innate desire to help and care for others can cause them to take advantage of you. Your partner is methodical, precise, grounded, and not easily fooled. They may view your generous expressions of love, care, and support as weak—on the surface, there is truth to that—you are likely too soft as a parent and too giving and forgiving—but on a deeper level, you have a strong core and the confidence that you can overcome anything.

You tend to avoid confrontations, especially with those you love. You prefer to support and love and let be. Your partner is a more hands-on parent who feels it's important to educate and discipline when needed.

You may feel, at times, that your partner is too controlling, and that may well be true, but keep in mind that this is due to their need to be protective—they see themselves as the guardian of the family. You are no less protective of those you love, but you show it with love and support. There can be times when you and your partner clash, when you feel their presence is limiting you, perhaps even in a claustrophobic way. It is important that when that happens, you communicate and don't let it fester.

The key to a successful relationship between you and your partner lies in tolerance and acceptance, to accept each other's differences and not to try to change each other.

Your partner is a 5

Your Life Path numbers may seem quite different, but they can complement each other well in a relationship. A person with a 5 Life Path can bring a sense of excitement and adventure to this partnership, while a person with a 6 Life Path can provide stability and emotional support.

Loving and caring for others is your most dominant trait, and you tend to attract a fair amount of attention from others who feel your love and want to be part of your life. Your partner also attracts others, but more due to their social and freewheeling lifestyle. For that reason, this can be a somewhat volatile match.

The powerful physical attraction between you and your partner is a source of strength and comfort for both of you because it makes you more secure and confident in the relationship. This is necessary, since there are other traits that are likely to be detrimental to your relationship. On top of that list would be jealousy, due to the plentiful attention you both get from others. You may, at times, feel your partner is somewhat superficial and maybe not as serious about the relationship as you would like them to be. When you think they are flirting, they are just being their usual charming self. You should know that the 5 Life Path is one of the most faithful and loyal people, whereas you, as a 6, are almost certainly more likely to stray. This is due to your innate nature of loving and caring, and sometimes, you might confuse someone's need for your love and support with a romantic need to love. This is a mistake that can put an end to the relationship.

An important issue you should be aware of is that your partner values freedom above anything else, and while this may sound contradictory to the earlier statement that, once committed, they are loyal and faithful, they do not take kindly to being restricted or limited in any way. Trust, therefore, is the most valuable commodity in your relationship. It is the only thing that stands between the potential of a lasting, truly satisfying and fulfilling relationship and a sudden and rather explosive breakup based on unsubstantiated suspicions and jealousy.

Ultimately, a successful relationship between you and your partner will require open communication, compromise, and a willingness to appreciate and respect each other's differences.

Your partner is a 6

As a rule, relationships fare better when the core numbers found in the same location of a chart are not the same. The 6 is an exception, largely because it is considered the most harmonious and committed of all numbers. You share the loving, caring qualities of a 6 Life Path: empathy, responsibility, dedication to the health and well-being of others, self-sacrifice, and the gift of counseling. You are the kind of person others come to in their moments of need. With those qualities abundantly present, your romantic relationship has an excellent chance of being fulfilling and lasting. Both of you are strongly committed and there is nothing you want more than to make your partner happy, and your partner feels the same way. You willingly sacrifice many of your own needs and desires for those of your partner, children, family, and friends.

However, there is a danger of devoting and sacrificing too much, and when that happens, helping becomes interfering, and advice and support turn into meddling in another person's life. There is a realistic danger of one or both of you becoming too involved with each other to the extent that you become intrusive, even suffocating. You must avoid a relationship based on codependency. It is important that you maintain your individuality and your ability to find happiness and contentment without relying solely on your partner, or anyone else for that matter. You may find that you spend every minute of every day together, and contrary to popular belief, that is not healthy, and it can cause resentment and frustration.

Another possible pitfall is unprovoked jealousy, an infliction that is not uncommon among those with a 6 Life Path. Relationships, romantic and otherwise, are extremely important to you, but you are not particularly good at reading subtle signs accurately. You may also tend to become a little possessive. Those qualities, combined with a sometimes overactive imagination (many artists have a 6 Life Path), can turn into jealousy, something you should guard against consciously. If you find yourself becoming suspicious of your partner with no obvious cause, step back and look at the situation as objectively as possible.

Every relationship has the potential of failure or of partners turning against each other for real or perceived reasons. The key to a long and happy relationship for two people with a 6 Life Path is to avoid misreading each other—in other words, communicate, especially if you experience doubt or confusion.

Your partner is a 7

A Life Path 6 and Life Path 7 often have a love-hate relationship, so it is uncommon to find it in romantic partners. While you are strongly committed and motivated by emotions and a need for romance, your partner is intellectual and somewhat secretive and distant. You need a strong physical and emotional connection; your partner seeks an intellectual bond and is less inclined to express their love as generously as you do. This has nothing to do with the ability or desire to love, since no number is more capable of loving than another, and the 7 is no exception. But challenges can arise when people have dramatically different views or strikingly different approaches to important concerns.

All numbers express love in a different way. You are mainly influenced by emotions, and you depend on expressions of love to feel safe and secure in a relationship. Your partner is more independent, which helps them to feel comfortable in a relationship even when deep personal feelings are not shared. Unless this fundamental difference is understood and accepted, it can become a problem in your relationship. You may, at times, feel your partner is cold and aloof and not as attentive as you would like them to be. Your partner needs some distance, space for quiet contemplation, daydreaming, and just being alone. When your partner is in that state of mind, even your loving attention could feel like an annoying disruption. When couples are unable to accept these differences, it can bring much unhappiness and cause arguments.

On a more promising note, there tends to be an intensity to the relationship between a 6 and a 7 that is largely due to a deep-seated desire to attain some of the qualities you see in each other. You love and admire your partner's intellectual and spiritual depth and it was almost certainly a major influence on your initial attraction. Similarly, deep down inside, your partner somewhat envies your easy dedication to other people's happiness or sorrows; they admire your warmth and generosity. For this reason, despite the many differences, this relation-ship may prove to be very strong. And although the differences are often obvious to others, they may go unnoticed by the two of you. People may wonder what keeps you together when you seem so different on all fronts.

You and your partner have the potential to create a happy, long-lasting relationship. The key is simply to recognize the fundamental dif-ference in the way you express your love. You must realize that even when your partner seems distant, your partner's love is not absent in any way. And your partner may have to recognize that you need fre-quent reassurance and will likely demand attention if you are remiss in demonstrating it.

Your partner is an 8

The Life Path number 6 is associated with love, family, and service, while the Life Path number 8 is associated with power, ambition, and success. When it comes to romantic compatibility between these two Life Path numbers, there can be some challenges due to their different approaches to life. However, there is also potential for a strong and com-plementary partnership.

You are both practical, goal-oriented people who are not afraid of responsibility. However, there are big differences in the way the 6 and 8 view responsibility, and an even bigger difference in the way they pursue their respective goals.

You are focused on family and friends and hesitant to do anything that could endanger the comfort and safety of your loved ones. Your partner's priority is fulfilling material goals and dreams. Where you will be reluctant to take risks that affect others, your partner doesn't hesitate to take risks to achieve their objective, because they feel it will benefit everyone's life if their material goals are met.

Interestingly, the 6 and 8 combination is excellent for business partnerships. Your partner inspires you to aim higher and seize opportunities, while you keep a rein on the dreams and vision of your partner to prevent them from taking unnecessary or misguided risks. However, without their ability to inspire, you might remain confined to smaller dreams requiring little or no risk. In other words, where your partner may reach too far, you like to play it safe; and while you may limit yourself, your partner will push you to see bigger visions. Still, without the grounded practicality of the 6, the 8 can get lost between creating the vision and achieving the goal.

In a romantic relationship, these numbers play off each other's strengths in similar ways that can be very beneficial. However, problems can arise if one partner tries to dominate the other. Your tendency to sacrifice and take on any burden, as well as your need to feel secure in a relationship, can put you at the mercy of your partner's perhaps overly assertive, even authoritarian and demanding nature. Sometimes, the opposite will happen, and your ability to make your partner feel guilty by simply demonstrating how much you are willing to do for them can diminish your partner's driven, focused energy.

The bottom line is that you have the potential to enhance each other's strengths and talents, or to create frustration and discord. The key to maintaining a rewarding, balanced relationship is to ensure neither of you dominate or shame the other.

Your partner is a 9

All numbers divisible by 3, such as your Life Path 6 and your partner's Life Path 9, have several things in common. First and foremost, they are sensitive to the physical, emotional, and spiritual needs of others. The 6 (you) expresses this in the love and care shown to family and friends. The 9 (your partner) directs their attention to the greater good—to humanity at large.

When the 6 and 9 are found between romantic partners, compatibility tends to be instant and permanent. Both of you are self-sacrificing, giving, and caring people. You are more practical while your partner is more idealistic, but your motivations are similar.

One attribute you share is your sense of justice; you both have a strong awareness of right and wrong. This could lead to one or both of you getting involved in politics or becoming activists or advocates for a cause. Unless you happen to be on opposing ends politically, this trait could further strengthen your bond.

Creativity and an eye for beauty are other aspects you have in common. Both you and your partner have artistic talents, especially in the visual area, like painting, sculpture, photography, interior or fashion design, architecture, and similar fields. Oddly, this is one of the few areas that can become a source of trouble. There will be times you have similar views when it comes to decorating, for example, but you will also often differ. When it comes to creative matters, you will both have strong opinions. In the event of a disagreement, you will need to compromise. Fortunately, that is something you are both quite capable of doing.

Although you are generally highly compatible, there are areas where you are likely to clash if certain negative traits are not acknowledged and kept under control. Although this is not common in your combination, it is something to be aware of. Your partner, although idealistic and self-sacrificing, has the potential to become somewhat aloof, arrogant, and self-righteous. Recognizing the relative value of your concepts and ideas may not be your partner's strong suit, which could lead to putting others down if they do not share your viewpoint.

If this tendency is combined with extreme religious belief, the 9 can become a negative influence on others, even destroying a relationship with the most devoted partner. Accepting that the "truth" as we understand it is relative allows us to have compassion and tolerance for others. The 9 is the least prejudiced of all numbers, so the likelihood of this being an issue is not high. But, as with all human traits, its dark side tends to be the direct opposite of its light side.

Although your 6 is considered the most loving of all numbers, it has a dark side as well. The 6 can become intolerant and angry, often without a clear cause. These negative emotions can fester, just waiting for the right opportunity to appear. The 6, although sincere, can also be intrusive and meddlesome to an uncomfortable degree.

The negative sides of the 6 and the 9 are rarely displayed, but you will need to be mindful that if they do raise their ugly heads, you will need to prevent them from spoiling what is most certainly one of the best relationship combinations around.

CHAPTER 7

Life Path 7

Your partner is a 1

You have a touch of the mystic, the hermit on the mountain, and you are not particularly concerned with seeing yourself as someone standing alone. Truth is, you often view yourself as apart from the rest of humanity, even to some extent your friends and family. It is therefore not easy for you to surrender yourself to feelings, whether romantic or otherwise. That does not mean you do not experience your emotions intensely and fully, because you certainly do, but you tend to hide them—often even from yourself—by analyzing them instead of appreciating them for what they are and what they give you. It is an interesting contradiction that you appreciate seeing others freely and confidently showing their feelings. It even makes you a little jealous, and you experience it as extremely attractive. The fact that your partner also has difficulty expressing their feelings therefore does nothing to strengthen the relationship. The weak spot in your relationship is most likely the lack of openly expressed and shared feelings.

Your partner has a strong, outspoken, and perhaps, at times, a little overbearing personality, and this is a source of both attraction and potential discord. It is important that you maintain your independence and to some extent even your privacy, and do not allow yourself to become too absorbed in your partner's world. If you leave it up to them, this could certainly become an issue, as they may have a tendency to control and dominate others, leading to potential problems. Once something or someone has become part of your partner's world, they will not easily let it go, and standing up to such a strong personality is not easy. As a result, you may find yourself turning away from their somewhat demanding and controlling manner.

Your relationship with your partner is based, in large part, on your shared interests and intellectual compatibility. You both like to wander off the beaten path and you are both unconventional, albeit in different ways. Your partner likes to look and act differently and probably enjoys being the cause of raised eyebrows and gossip. There is a bit of a rebel in them. In the early stages of the relationship, this is another source of mutual attraction; however, your partner will likely try to shape you in their image and that is something you want to avoid.

You have many traits in common, but they tend to express themselves differently. You are both intensely curious, but while you approach the unknown intellectually, your partner thrives on action. People with a 1 Life Path are explorers and adventurers. Those with a 7 Life Path are researchers and thinkers. Similarly, you are both emotionally distant, again for different reasons. You simply don't trust emotions; you rely on the mind to guide you and give you clarity. This is something you may want to consider, because the bottom line is that feelings are more powerful than logic. When it comes to life's challenges and opportunities, the heart is the greatest motivator.

Your partner often views feelings, at least showing them, as a weakness. They are courageous on the physical plane, they are warriors and will stand up for what they believe in, but that bravery is lacking when it comes to the emotional plane. As mentioned earlier, feelings are the weak spot in this relationship, but that can be remedied by making the conscious decision to express and share your feelings. You may even want to consider setting a specific time or opportunity aside, perhaps with a glass of wine or just holding hands, to devote yourself to the honest and brave act of sharing emotions. It is guaranteed to make your relationship stronger and more enjoyable.

Your partner is a 2

This is a rare combination in romantic relationships. Friendship or business relationships are more common among these extremely different Life Paths. However, when a 7 Life Path is romantically involved with a 2 Life Path, it can produce a uniquely beautiful partnership—only after some major hurdles have been overcome.

First and foremost is your almost detached approach to romance. You are highly mental, you think and analyze and try to find reason in everything, even romance. You may want to discuss it, classify it, judge it, and compartmentalize it. You are not particularly good at simply expressing it. You can look in your partner's eyes and see the love, because they will reach out physically and emotionally to manifest their feelings. You are not as emotionally available, and that can be a big challenge to your partner. It is important that you learn to express your feelings without hesitation and without trying to hide behind words and superficial physical expressions. This not only greatly empowers the relationship, but it will also, without a doubt, make you a happier and more fulfilled person, regardless of relationships.

A word of caution; your partner is highly intuitive and sensitive and is vulnerable to harsh words and criticism. You should be careful in how you handle discord or disagreements. While their love is strong and easily expressed, they can turn on a dime and walk away if they are treated badly. They are not victims. They are survivors, so keep that in mind.

Your partner is more intuitive than most people and will see your love and know you are capable of loving deeply and your loyalty is second to none, but they also see your reluctance in expressing it without inhibition. You are, after all, a bit of a stranger in the world of feelings—you are not at home there, because they confuse you and pull you out of your comfort zone. You would do well to consciously work on expressing your feelings, something that requires great courage, but also offers great rewards. Your challenge is to be less intimidated by the gentle power of love and romance, and more uninhibited in expressing yourself. It will enrich your life tremendously and almost guarantee that your relationship has longevity.

If you can show your partner your love and devotion instead of just speaking words to that effect, you will have captured their heart forever. Your partner is a master in subtlety and can read your heart better than you do, so you might as well trust your love and jump in with both feet.

Your partner is a 3

You are a seeker, intellectually curious, and always looking for deeper meaning. Your partner is playful, creative, upbeat, and impulsive. You are serious and a bit of a dreamer. Your partner keeps things light and on the surface. This is a relationship that either crashes in its early stages or lasts for a lifetime. If you want it to last, you will need to accept your partner's apparently superficial approach to pretty much everything and avoid feeling superior because you tend to look deeper and are more analytical.

Your partner has an intuitive understanding and connection with reality that allows them to float through life with less drama than most people, but make no mistake, they are no less involved and affected by the events and circumstances than you are. For them, the glass is always half-full even when it's almost empty, while you tend to be more pessimistic and often plagued by self-doubt.

You must recognize that your partner's playful approach to life does not reflect a shallow person—their depth is hiding behind a smile and a joke. In fact, your partner might be more challenged to accept you as you are, because they know that you hide a big part of yourself. You have a secretive nature and are not given to show your deeper feelings or fears. It is difficult for your partner to accept that barrier because they don't hide their feelings—they are out in the open, camouflaged perhaps by their lighthearted nature, but look beyond the smile and you sense an intensity of feeling and an emotional awareness.

You are both unconventional and a bit of a mystery to your friends and family. You are different, and yet also alike. When a 3 and a 7 build a life together and it survives the early years, the connection is stronger than most relationships and often almost uncanny in how you may finish each other's sentences or understand exactly what your partner thinks with a single glance. This is precisely because you needed to reach deep and listen hard to each other in the early years to reach that level of acceptance and understanding. Only love can do that.

Your partner is a 4

You are very different, especially in your outlook on life, how you want to live, and in the way you think, and there are certainly a few areas in which you may have potential conflict. However, this is a very promising relationship that easily grows deep and permanent roots.

You are drawn to the esoteric, the abstract, the world of thought and dreams, while your partner is grounded and practical. Your partner is your anchor, and this creates a nice balance; your partner is introduced to your expansive inner world where ideas float like balloons, while they try to prevent you from your tendency to try to fly the same iron balloon over and over. Your partner is a realist, and you are a dreamer. Communication is an important part of any relationship, but in yours it is more than that; you feed off of each other, and you will likely never tire of your partner's solid, pragmatic response to your lofty dreams and out-of-the-box ideas.

It is likely that you were drawn to each other from an early age and were comfortable with each other almost from day one. It might have been love at first sight, and it probably didn't take more than two or three occasions to realize you wanted to be with them for the rest of your life. Curiosity and a feeling of being safe and protected were a big part of it, more than a physical attraction. This is especially true for your partner. You wanted to know what kind of world your partner lived in, how they felt and thought and managed to maintain such a solid, calm disposition. Your partner saw in you a reflection of the mystery of life, not unlike how you might view a bearded mystic in a mountain cave: "Who is this person, and what kind of world do they live in?"

We are drawn to the unknown if it feels safe, and we fear the unknown if it doesn't. Between you and your partner, there is some of that; you feel safe, but also sense that if you get too close, you might lose your freedom. Your partner is attracted to the lack of limitations in thought and perhaps even action that you represent, but they also fear that freedom as it represents a lack of rules and boundaries, which are such a big part of who they are; they thrive on them.

If you and your partner can walk that fine line between freedom and commitment, if you continue to appreciate their earthly, grounded nature, and they don't lose their attraction to your inquisitive, free-wheeling mind, this relationship could be exciting and rewarding for a long time.

Your partner is a 5

There are strengths and challenges in your relationship, but you and your partner will find that you are generally very compatible. You are often introspective and analytical, and you enjoy exploring deep philosophical and spiritual questions. You are drawn to intellectual pursuits and may have a natural talent for research or analysis.

Your partner, on the other hand, is more spontaneous and adventurous. They are quite social and enjoy meeting new people and experiencing new things. They have a natural talent for communication and are very persuasive or charming. You are a deep thinker, while your partner has a more sparkling and excitable mind.

When these two numbers come together in a relationship, there is a good balance of intellectual stimulation and excitement. You provide the depth and introspection needed to explore deep spiritual or philosophical questions, while your partner's dynamic energy brings a sense of adventure and spontaneity to the relationship.

You are a thinker, a searcher; you have depth, and you are not much for chitchat. That's why some people who know you are surprised that you're connected with a 5, but it's a good match. Your partner can think on their feet and quickly and they have a curious mind and are easily excitable, which can be inspiring and stimulating.

However, there may also be some challenges to overcome. You can sometimes be seen as too serious or detached, which may clash with your partner's more lighthearted and social nature. They need to feel that you are involved and that you appreciate their effort to draw you into their world. Your partner can sometimes be scattered or inconsistent, which may be frustrating to you since you tend to be more focused and deliberate in your thinking.

Another area of potential trouble is that your partner is more physical and sensual and expresses their love generously, verbally and through touch. You tend to be more distant, but that is due to the fact that a serious mind tends to be inhibited and has a more difficult time letting go and just enjoying the moment. Your love is no less deep and committed; you are just not as comfortable letting it show.

Your relationship has an above average chance of bringing happiness and lasting a lifetime, in large part because while you are intellectually and emotionally very different, you complement each other well. If you can allow yourself to be more generous and verbal about your love for your partner, it would strengthen the relationship significantly.

Your partner is a 6

You are more reserved and inward-focused than your partner. Their 6 Life Path tells you they are dedicated to family and friends, they are very involved in the lives of those close to them, and while you are not any less capable of loving and caring, you tend to be more private.

Your partner requires a physical and emotional connection, while your love relationship is more based on an intellectual bond. This has nothing to do with the ability or desire to love, since no number is more capable of loving than any other. But challenges can arise when people have dramatically different views or strikingly different approaches to important concerns.

All numbers express love in a different way. Your partner's 6 is largely influenced by emotions and depends on expressions of love to feel safe and secure in a relationship. Your 7 is more independent, which enables you to feel comfortable in a relationship even when deep personal feelings are not often shared.

Unless this fundamental difference is understood and accepted, it can become a problem in your relationship. Your partner may, at times, feel that you are cold and aloof, and not as attentive as they would like. You need a certain amount of distance, space for quiet contemplation, daydreaming, and just being alone. When you are in that state of mind, even your partner's loving attention can feel like an annoying disruption.

When couples are unable to accept these diverging viewpoints and approaches, it can bring much unhappiness. Interestingly, despite these contrasts, the relationship often remains unbreakable—in part due to the loyalty and patience of your partner, but you also tend to be loyal, and most importantly, your intuitive understanding of the human psyche makes you quite forgiving.

The key to a long and loving relationship for you and your partner is simply to recognize the fundamental difference in the way you express your love. Your partner must realize that even when you seem distant, your love is not absent in any way. And you may have to accept the fact that your partner needs frequent reassurance, and you should be willing to put your reluctance to be emotionally available aside and pay attention and give your love. It can be extremely helpful if you occasionally can go out of your way to show your love—with flowers or chocolate or an action that clearly shows your willingness to sacrifice what you want to give your partner what they need.

Your partner is a 7

Yours is a beautiful combination, with great potential for spiritual growth. Both of you appreciate life and life's mysteries deeply. You have a strong intellectual and spiritual bond and thrive on each other's intellect and wisdom.

The relationship between the 7 and 7 may begin in the heart, but it quickly moves to the inner realms. The term *soulmates* applies to couples who share a 7 Life Path. Poets at heart—even if you have never written a poem in your life—you intuitively recognize that your bond with each other is spiritual in nature and more valuable than anything else in your lives. You grow together, without the need to constantly be together. You probably communicate in half sentences and often find yourself thinking or expressing the same thing your partner just said—even early in the relationship.

If your relationship is moving toward maturity, you are likely to be "joined at the hip." That said, there are also things to watch for to avoid spoiling such a beautiful relationship. No other number can, at times, become as stubborn and unforgiving, even in small matters. In extreme cases, the 7 can become small-minded, even neurotic. While rare, a tendency to allow a minor issue to become a major disagreement does exist. What is interesting is that important issues rarely cause the same reaction; you are too intelligent to be petty. But the same person who can lead a study group with insight and who has the ability to communicate even the most arcane concepts can turn into a hairsplitter when it comes to seemingly minor household issues.

There is one issue you should be particularly aware of, as it has the potential to destroy this otherwise excellent combination. You both enjoy a highly imaginative inner life. Consequently, you need time alone for study, contemplation, or just to let your mind wander. When your living space is too small, or you lead hectic lives continually surrounded by others—even each other—your need for quiet personal space will begin to take precedence over everything else. It is not uncommon for people with a 7 Life Path to leave a promising career, relationship, or family due to this inner need. It is important that you find a way to honor this and create an environment where you can have time alone. If you become aware of underlying tension building, talk to your partner and discuss solutions. Recognize your common need to share your life and ideas while maintaining your individuality and need for personal space and time.

Your partner is an 8

A Life Path 7 and a Life Path 8 are usually not attracted to each other or particularly compatible in romantic relationships, except the purely physical aspect—this can be a strong motivator but is usually not enough to make the relationship last. The notion that opposites attract does not generally hold true here.

This does not mean you cannot have a fulfilling, well-suited relationship. However, you have major differences in your personal makeup that can cause problems—in fact, you are basically on opposite ends of the spectrum in almost all areas. If the relationship has been in place for a year or longer, and is currently strong and positive, you likely overcame some stressful episodes with mutual love and communication, which is as promising as it is unusual for these two numbers, as neither one is good at sharing feelings.

Your priorities differ. Your partner has a strong drive for financial success and security. For you, spiritual and intellectual growth is a higher priority. Your partner intuitively understands the balance between the material and intangible, which is the reason they excel in business, marketing, or sales. (One must be somewhat detached from material gain to have the vision and clarity it takes to be successful in business.)

You move in the inner realms and are not drawn to business, even, deep down, deeming it unworthy of attention. You would rather discuss political, philosophical, or spiritual matters, with a preference for the abstract—issues that could seem boring to your partner who prefers a practical, down-to-earth approach that focuses on results.

Similarly, you could find yourselves at opposite ends of the spectrum when it comes to likes and dislikes, from movies to books, travel to housing, decorating, art, and so forth. You might enjoy living in a rather isolated, cozy country home, while your partner would be happy in a futuristic loft in a large metropolis. The friends you attract will also be quite different. You prefer quiet conversations rather than loud parties. Your partner enjoys a more energetic environment and interaction with others.

The potential lack of compatibility between these numbers has nothing to do with the heart. It generally involves practical preferences, such as where to live, how to decorate the house, and who you become friends with. This can be overcome by allowing each other considerable space and freedom in the way you live your lives. You will both need to recognize and accept your differences.

The key to a successful relationship for this unusual match is communication, respect, and a willingness to live and let live. A little distance in many areas is not a bad thing for a 7 and an 8 Life Path—you both need space, and neither one of you needs someone to tell you how you should live your life—and that includes each other.

Your partner is a 9

It is not that common for a Life Path 7 and a Life Path 9 to be in romantic relationships, or any other relationship for that matter. It is not that they don't get along—they usually get along well if there is not too much interaction, and yes, that sounds like an oxymoron. However, while they are compatible in some areas, they are generally not that interested in each other's issues, hobbies, interests, and so forth. If you imagine the 7 and 9 as two archetypes forced to spend time together at a social event, you will witness them politely, although superficially, chatting for a few minutes, then running out of things to talk about and lapsing into silence. They do not dislike each other; they just do not share common interests.

When a 7 and a 9 become involved with each other, it is generally a powerful physical attraction and, more importantly, because they recognize one commonality they share, one that can be enough to sustain a relationship. You both like to live independently and in a kind of personal and private bubble, although for different reasons. You, with a 7 Life Path, are unconventional and inward focused with a very active imagination—you are an observer who is less inclined to mingle in social settings than to stand somewhat aside and watch the show. Your partner will mingle, motivated in large part by their innate curiosity about how people think and what makes them tick, but to most people they will still appear somewhat distant. Put both of you in a relationship of any kind, and there is a deep understanding acknowledging each other's need for space and privacy that can become a solid basis for the relationship, but to those around you, you seem to live separate lives.

Religion is one area where the 7 and the 9 tend to be incompatible. Your partner thrives on faith and has the intuitive understanding that things are already in balance without the need to manipulate them. You, on the other hand, use logic and reason and do not accept things at face value. You question everything, and the notion of "belief" is alien to your intellectual quest for understanding.

Your differing tastes may generate other areas of conflict. Your partner might prefer to live in a large city, while a cozy chalet in the countryside would be paradise for you. (Helpful hint: when it comes to choosing colors and furnishings for the home, your partner is probably better suited to the task.) Every number combination has challenges. Yours will likely revolve around differing interests and your contrasting views on issues that arise.

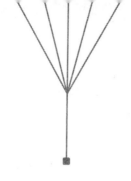

CHAPTER 8

Life Path 8

Your partner is a 1

You and your partner have quite a few traits in common, some that strengthen the relationship, and some that do not. You both are highly motivated in all areas of life; you are competitive and goal-oriented. For that reason, your relationship is well suited to sharing a business or some other venture, if your roles are carefully separated. You do not want to get in each other's way, because neither one of you will back down. In your relationship with your partner, you must be prepared to occasionally play second fiddle, and that is not something that comes natural to you. It will therefore have to be a conscious effort.

As a person with an 8 Life Path, you are likely to be a domineering presence in most social settings—you enjoy being the center of attention, but your partner will either compete for that role or resent you for it, because they too like the limelight. So be on guard for this potential issue, and when you sense this may be the case, just wander off and find another group to entertain.

You and your partner desire the better things in life. Status is important for both of you, and you like to flaunt what you have. For that reason, a relationship between a 1 and an 8 can become financially stressful if there is no restraint on spending, even though you are both likely to do well financially.

Another trait you share that does not help the relationship is that patience is not your forte, nor your partner's. In addition, you are both quick to point out the other person's faults. Add the fact that neither one of you is particularly tactful, and it is a recipe for a rather turbulent relationship.

At this point, you may have concluded that the relationship between an 8 and a 1 is challenging, and that is certainly true. However, both you and your partner are extremely loyal and capable of absorbing multiple blows without going down. You are both resilient, and while there are almost certainly going to be explosive arguments, neither one of you carries a grudge and you will be able to make up and move on.

The key to a happy and lasting relationship between an 8 and a 1 is a willingness to express and share your feelings—again, not something either of you is good at. You would benefit greatly if you made a conscious effort to let your partner know what is going on with you, and to ask the same from them. If you can share and communicate your feelings, your relationship may be turbulent at times, but it has an excellent chance of lasting and enriching your life.

Your partner is a 2

Your Life Path number is dramatically different from your partner, but they are not incompatible. In fact, your differences complement each other well: you are the result-oriented go-getter; you live to move forward and onward, to whatever is next over the horizon. You don't spend a lot of time in contemplation or working on your emotional well-being.

Your partner is intuitive, sensitive, emotional, and capable of recognizing the subtle signs we transmit as human beings. Your partner reads you better than you read them, and that is a good thing, especially if you can be humble enough to listen and take their words to heart.

This relationship has the potential to be long-lasting and joyful if you give each other room to be who you are. It is also important that you do not underestimate your partner—something people tend to do to those born with a 2 Life Path. This would be a mistake, because while they appear gentle, tactful, accommodating, and willing to bend to the will of others, they do not break, and during hardship or stressful times, they will outlive just about anyone else. They are not the rock people lean on, they are the rope that won't break and pulls others to safety.

You are an entrepreneur at heart. You are a visionary and highly focused on material success. You exude authority and leadership, and your partner appreciates that. However, even those with an 8 Life Path can reach bottom when things don't work out, and you may feel victimized and blame the world. It is important that you always look at yourself first, find the cause of a failure, and realize that it is only temporary and that you can change and grow.

Your partner can be a pillar of support during those times, especially if they see the fighter spirit in you. They are very sensitive and capable of recognizing subtle signs that escape most people, but they have come to know you and fallen in love with you in part because they admire that strength. While they will accept moments of weakness in others, they will have difficulty accepting it from you, because they expect to see you strong and authoritative. They put the bar higher for you, and hope you can live up to that. If you can, you will have their love and admiration for life, and your relationship will be stronger for it. But your partner understands human nature better than most and they will be there for you during times when you simply have run out of steam or need a shoulder to lean on.

Your partner is a 3

You are driven and ambitious and will pursue a goal until you reach your desired outcome. You are quite serious about your endeavors and focused on tangible results.

Your partner is creative and can think out of the box but is not as focused as you are. They see life more as a play, as something that should be enjoyed. Therefore, when a project becomes too cumbersome, or they simply lose interest, they will drop it and move on to something else. It can be irritating, and it is your challenge to accept your partner for who they are. Unfortunately, that does not come naturally to you.

Although you take differing approaches, you are both energetic and capable of turning dreams into reality. Quite often, this combination is seen between business partners or longtime friends who start a business together. In that environment, your partner would be the initial creative source, while you would be the visionary, planner, and organizer. Together, you could do very well.

You would do well to remember that while your partner generally seems to take things lightheartedly, going about their day with smiles and jokes, there are times when that is nothing more than a cover-up for emotional turmoil and heartache. It is difficult to know when their upbeat nature is real and when it isn't. The sensitivity and intuitive intelligence needed to recognize what your partner is really experiencing is not your forte, so you need to pay close attention and never take their joyful attitude for granted.

Another possible source of contention can be your inborn sense of authority, both in accepting it and applying it. This is entirely alien to your more freewheeling, happy-go-lucky partner. Any attempt to control them or push them in a direction they don't want to go is bound to create major discord. This can be frustrating to you, because you don't feel that anything worthwhile can be accomplished without discipline and single-minded focus. Your partner, on the other hand, thrives on a little chaos; it brings out their creativity. Your partner will always be playful, perhaps even a little childlike, but keep in mind that when push comes to shove, they know what they want and they will not tolerate another person's interference, even those they love.

This is not an easy combination. However, if the relationship has existed for at least a few years, it may well last a lifetime because the initial attraction—for you, their sunny, optimistic bearing, and for them, your strong and powerful focus—will never change.

Your partner is a 4

An 8 Life Path and a 4 Life Path can build one of the most promising relationships, because while vastly different, they are compatible and complement each other well.

You are both practical and capable of setting goals and reaching them. You are a leader and a visionary, ambitious and confident. You are a planner, but you tend to skip over the details. Your partner is hard-working, reliable, methodical, and detail-oriented. This is an excellent combination for business. But you also have the qualities needed to make a romantic relationship work.

Neither one of you is particularly amorous—you are too grounded for that—but you tend to have an easygoing camaraderie you both enjoy.

One potential area of friction is that you are very independent and tend to struggle with emotional intimacy. Your partner, while not as inhibited as you are, is not particularly sensitive or tuned in to the inner world of feelings either. As a result, although you know that they are loyal to a fault, there are times when you feel distant, and the relationship feels more like a friendship than a romance. You should both work consciously on keeping the romance alive and sparkling. Schedule date nights or quiet evenings at home specifically to feel close and to talk about what goes on with you on a deeper level.

As mentioned, you are a visionary—you have ideas and goals and big dreams, often in business but also in other areas, but you don't always consider all the details. You don't have time for that. Your partner is the one who will see the details and is more pragmatic. This blend of traits can cause friction if one isn't willing to listen to the other, and vice versa. The 8 Life Path intuitively understands the balance between the material and the spiritual; you can pursue worldly dreams with complete dedication and yet be detached from the financial reward, at least to the extent you are willing to take hard-earned financial gains and risk them in another venture, a risk your partner will not be comfortable with.

By the same token, you can experience frustration with your partner's need to approach a project carefully, to analyze each step and find potential problems you are not interested in hearing about. In the practical world, it is important that you show mutual respect and listen to each other. This is not always easy and gets more difficult as time goes by, because familiarity can breed contempt, and that, in turn, makes it harder to accept or even be open to the other's thoughts.

Another possible point of conflict can be that you are by nature a bit of an authoritarian. Initially, your partner will likely accept and perhaps barely notice this trait in you, but over time it can become a problem. You must see your partner as an equal, not someone to dominate, because it will ruin the relationship in a hurtful way. This is even more important because neither one of you is particularly romantic, and you both tend to keep emotional expressions of love to a minimum. But your partner needs to hear them and needs regular confirmation that they are loved. If you do that, the relationship has an excellent chance of enduring many ups and downs.

Your partner is a 5

You are a doer, a visionary, and quite serious about making your life story one of success, both in accomplishments and in the accumulation of wealth. You are not a dreamer; you plan, set your goals, and don't stop until you have reached them.

Your partner is different; they are spontaneous, adventurous, and somewhat chaotic in their approach to everything from career to lifestyle, and even romance. Your partner is quick-witted and can think on their feet. They are sociable and easygoing and tend to change career and goals easily. This difference can cause problems, as you may feel they are unfocused and undisciplined—and there is some truth to that. However, you must accept that this is their nature, and it usually works well for them. They are adaptable and good at grabbing opportunities when they arise. They don't hesitate, and this is a quality that makes you nervous. While you have a better than average sense of business and are perfectly willing to take calculated risks, the key word here is *calculated*. You don't trust your partner's quick decisions and their often radical and unexpected changes. You are more deliberate and like to think things through. It is important that you don't try to change or slow your partner down. And your partner should realize that while you are slower and more careful, that often translates into winning formulas, as you are almost certainly better than your partner at making ideas turn into reality and getting rewarded financially and in other ways for your well-planned endeavors.

One area where you might find that you can improve is in the way you express your love and commitment. Your partner is quite sensual and will usually be the first to reach out. However, they need attention, and they need to feel that their love is fully reciprocated. They are, as mentioned earlier, quite sociable and are comfortable being the center of attention, which may sometimes cause you some dismay. But while they may seem erratic and sometimes even flirty (they are very charming and not always able to set the limits of social interactions where you would expect them to be), those with a 5 Life Path are the most loyal and committed romantic partners; they are the least likely to cheat, and a part of them is always aware that you are there, and that you are the one they want to be with. For your partner, freedom is crucial, so you can be assured that when they commit, and thereby surrender some of their freedom, they do so consciously and totally.

Your relationship can be pleasant and long-lasting, but you will probably need to be realistic about your expectations and maintain some distance in your lifestyles and day-to-day routines. Your key to a successful relationship lies in giving each other space and freedom—you do not want to smother your partner or be overly protective; they don't need it and don't want it.

Your partner is a 6

You and your partner complement each other well in a romantic relationship since you both have a strong desire for success and achievement, although you approach it from different angles. You are driven to succeed and are a visionary—you consider material wealth to be the foundation of a successful relationship, and you are willing to provide just that. Your partner is more focused on the emotional connection and may, at times, feel that you are too involved in your career or business and don't pay enough attention to their needs or the needs of other family members. They may struggle to understand your focus on material possessions and financial success, and it may be helpful if they would recognize that much of your motivation and effort comes from your desire to make yourself and others happy—as you can see, you both have a different take on what it means to have a long and loving relationship, but the goal is the same.

Therefore, your willingness to communicate openly and support each other's needs is crucial to the relationship. With understanding, you can build a strong and fulfilling relationship based on mutual respect and a single shared goal.

There are other areas where you are quite different yet share a desire for the same outcome. You are both practical, goal-oriented people who are not afraid of responsibility. However, there are big differences in the way you and your partner view responsibility, and an even bigger difference in the way you pursue your respective goals. Your partner is focused on family and friends, and is hesitant to do anything that could endanger the comfort and safety of their loved ones. Your priority is fulfilling material goals and dreams. Where your partner will be reluctant to take risks that affect others, you won't hesitate to take risks to achieve your objective, because you feel it will benefit everyone.

In a romantic relationship, these numbers play off each other's strengths in ways that can be very beneficial but can also cause problems. You have a strong, even authoritarian personality and may be tempted to dominate your partner, whose tendency to sacrifice and take on any burden can put them at the mercy of your somewhat assertive and demanding nature.

By the same token, your partner may use their tendency to sacrifice as a tool to make you feel guilty. Neither one of these scenarios will help the relationship, and when you recognize that perhaps one or the other is in play, you should take time to communicate and to relay your worries. It is crucial in this relationship that one does not attempt to dominate the other. You are both quite self-sufficient and the feeling that you are being controlled or manipulated will be detrimental to an otherwise promising relationship.

Your partner is a 7

You are pragmatic, a visionary, decisive, a result-oriented go-getter. Your partner is more subdued, a thinker, a dreamer, skeptical, and distant. When romance blooms between an 8 and a 7, the initial attraction tends to be physical, combined with a sense of curiosity from both sides. Two quite different people trying to enter each other's worlds, but each approaching it differently.

Your partner can spend hours talking about the universe, or life, and while they do most of the talking, their penetrating eyes are busy searching; they are feeling you out, and they are good at it. Not much escapes them, and they are excellent interrogators. However, when it comes to matters of the heart, they flounder. You may find your partner difficult to reach, because most 7s are emotionally insecure. It is a part of them they are not entirely comfortable with; they thrive on logic, common sense, and self-control. Feelings do not support self-control, and that scares them. This is also the reason it takes time before they trust enough to allow their sensual side to come out and play. They feel very strongly, and sensuality plays a big role in their lives, but they do not surrender to their feelings easily. For that reason, in the early stages of a romance between you and your partner, you would do well to show patience and sensitivity—neither one of which, unfortunately, are your forte. You are ready to take the plunge and let your feelings control your decisions, and you are not afraid to merge and share. You are a strong presence in most social settings, and that includes romance. You are equally happy to take control, to offer your heart to the person who caught your eye.

Your partner will always spend much of their time in their inner world of thought. This is who they are, and while a romance may temporarily reach a stage of almost complete submission to the excitement of love and being in love, the love may last but the submission will not.

They will always be a little distant, hiding a part of themselves. They are private and sometimes even secretive, not because their love is less powerful, but because they treasure their inner world more than most people. That is where they like to dwell. You, on the other hand, are comfortable and secure looking outside and reacting to whatever happens to be going on, in real time. You are more direct, and in the eyes of your partner, quite fearless. You do not have that mental buffer that needs a nanosecond to digest and seek the hidden reality behind everything before responding.

Your relationship is challenging, but it is also passionate and potentially long-lasting if you can allow your partner to keep some emotional distance and have a more private, inner world. While your love burns quick and hot, your partner's love has a slower start but will grow and continue to grow. Once your partner trusts you, you will have a lover and a friend for life.

Your partner is an 8

You are well suited to support each other's endeavors, as well as start a venture together. You are both visionaries with imagination and a talent for business. However, you are also both driven to be in charge, and you do not like to surrender control. This may cause you to become competitive, which could lead to jealousy or anger. But if you direct your competitive natures against other forces, you have a good chance of a long and happy relationship, with the potential for financial prosperity as well. In general, this combination creates excellent friendships, sometimes a great business relationship, but not usually a romance—so yours is rare. If a romance does happen between two people with an 8 Life Path, it is often short-lived or it lasts a lifetime—there does not seem to be a middle road. Fortunately, there are ways to increase the chance of making your relationship happy and lasting. Most important, if you share a business or some other endeavor and you find that you compete or disagree to an extent that anger and frustration rear their ugly heads, one of you should get out. It is a clear indicator that, as far as career and business, you need to go your separate ways.

Another possible pitfall is that while the 8 is a good number for business, its tendency to risk everything in pursuit of a dream could bring either tremendous success or total loss. No other number is willing to ride a financial roller coaster like the 8. You will need to keep an eye on each other to prevent extreme risk-taking. An 8 Life Path does not easily accept responsibility for failure of any kind, which is why the harmony and happiness in your relationship depends in large part on financial stability. Although an 8 will accept risks and can put up with financial ups and downs when they are alone, in a partnership they tend to put the blame on their partner, which can cause friction. Being financially strapped will negatively impact all other areas of your shared life as well. Within the context of a romantic relationship, it is important that you follow your natural inclination to pursue success, but it is equally important that you keep enough of your assets safely set aside to avoid serious problems.

The 8 thrives on their sense of authority, and both of you understand that need, particularly when it comes to raising children; however, this may lead to you being more controlling than most parents, which could be another source of trouble. When both parents tend to create environments where children are given everything they need, but this is accompanied by too much control, it will cause disharmony in the family and conflict between you and your partner. Neither one of you will easily accept responsibility when your children rebel. It is quite common for children with one or more parents with an 8 Life Path to push back against authority. It is important that you understand your authoritative nature and recognize that your partner—and children—have their own paths to forge.

Your partner is a 9

The 8 and 9 have almost nothing in common and are not considered particularly compatible, yet they are often strongly attracted to each other—in this case, opposites attract. Interestingly, this attraction can remain compelling and fresh for many years because there is always something new to discover in each other.

A go-getter with big dreams and expectations, you have a good chance to turn many of those dreams into reality because you are highly motivated and willing to put forth enormous effort to reach a goal. It is in your nature to direct energy toward accumulating wealth and power, so for you, this is natural and healthy.

Your partner is equally focused, but driven by completely different priorities and motives. Your partner is motivated by the work itself and the way it affects the lives of others, rather than financial gain or material success. Your partner finds personal reward when driven by humanitarian motives, while you find happiness in seeing tangible rewards.

Obviously, your priorities are as different as night and day, yet both are as they should be. You will often find yourselves at opposite sides of a discussion and will rarely agree when it comes to practical matters, but your mutual respect and love makes this possible without turning it into a major source of discontent.

For a happy relationship, you both will need to recognize and respect your differences. If you take each other for granted or begin to feel you can predict and control your partner, your relationship will be in trouble. The key word in this relationship is *respect*. If you respect each other, disagreements—of which there will probably be many—will not weaken your foundation.

CHAPTER 9

Life Path 9

Your partner is a 1

You have chosen a partner who is radically different from you. You are an idealist, a bit of a dreamer, and someone who wants to believe in justice and fairness and equality, while your partner is a doer, a real go-getter, with little time or patience for dreamers. The attraction originated most likely in the few traits you do share.

You are both creative, unconventional, and willing to take risks. Your partner appreciates your sense of humor, while you are attracted to their devil-may-care attitude. Aside from those shared traits, you and your partner view reality from entirely different angles and often find that you cannot relate to each other. You also must accept that your partner is not a patient person and that communication can be difficult because you like to go into a subject in depth, probing around until you feel you understand it correctly. Your partner drills down to the core and comes back with strong opinions and little room for discussion. Listening to each other should therefore be a conscious effort.

Ironically, although it presents challenges, this is not a bad combination for most other types of relationships. Friendships, parent-child, and business relationships often work very well in this combination precisely because the numbers stand on opposite ends of the spectrum. They complement and balance each other. Together, they offer a range of talents and useful qualities that enhance most relationships, but romance—not so much. For that reason, you would do well giving each other space, and do not try to change your partner's mind; it will not work.

Your partner can be confrontational and tends to be quite opinionated. Standing up to that when you are not in agreement is challenging for you, and there is a danger of becoming somewhat apathetic and surrendering to their sometimes overbearing personality. Over time, this would turn into resentment and eventually a painful breakup.

To create a harmonious, long-term relationship, you will need to leave each other be, especially during the first couple of years. If your relationship survives three or four years and there is still a powerful attraction, it may well last a lifetime.

Your partner is a 2

Generally, the 2 Life Path and 9 Life Path do not get along easily. Your focus is on the world at large. You are an idealist. Your partner is more emotionally involved and focuses on forming a deep, cooperative relationship with people close to them. Interestingly, the 2 and the 9 can form powerful alliances in other circumstances, particularly business.

Your partner is open and easygoing in matters of the heart, while you are more careful and perhaps somewhat distant. It is helpful if your partner recognizes and accepts your need to maintain some distance, because if your partner pushes too fast and too hard, it may turn you off—especially in the early stages of your relationship. This would be unfortunate, because your partner can loosen your inhibitions and create a comfort zone where you can feel at ease and secure. Their inborn sensitivity and innate awareness of other people's feelings are just what you need to experience that level of freedom and passion all humans crave.

But it will not be an easy path. Your partner is almost certainly more passionate and physical in their expressions of love and attraction, and while this kind of early romantic enthusiasm has caused you to back off and even break off relationships in the past, you would do well to be more flexible and accepting within this partnership, because there is a lot of promise and potential. All you need to do is give yourself and your partner time.

You are more inhibited and distant than most people, although this inhibition can express itself in different ways. You may see yourself as affectionate and even passionate, but it is typical of a 9 Life Path to come off as hard to reach and read, even while expressing your love physically. Expressing yourself emotionally is particularly difficult to you—you are uncomfortable making yourself vulnerable. It is a trait that may well escape you, but your partner will feel that, and it can be troubling to them.

Your partner is just the opposite. Feeling safe and comfortable comes easily to them, even early on in a relationship. They are naturally more optimistic about romance, as they are in all matters of the heart. This may seem like a contradiction, since they are known to be sensitive and vulnerable, but they are also aware of their resilience—deep down they know that while they may be the first one to feel hurt and broken, they are also the first to be back on their feet and continue their journey.

Difficulties may arise when the relationship becomes more physical and intimate, as it touches a deeper part of you. It is in your nature, in any relationship, be it friends or coworkers or lovers, to maintain a little distance. You feel safe because you don't have to rely on trust. Your partner is different and will invite you to share even your deepest feelings. It is up to you to share that desire and to overcome your inhibitions in that respect, because it will greatly strengthen and deepen your relationship.

Your partner is a 3

The 9 and the 3 are one of the more promising combinations with a potential to form a strong and lasting bond. Your patience and tolerance toward each other is legendary.

Your partner's sense of humor and sunny disposition make them the light of the party and often the center of attention. You, on the other hand, prefer to be the observer, and will tend to keep some distance. You must be careful not to become insecure or ignored due to your partner's popularity. They enjoy the limelight, but they know that you are their safe haven and the temporary excitement being the center of attention does not prevent them from knowing who they want to be with at the end of the day.

You are more focused and efficient than your partner. You are an idealist, but you are not a dreamer, and you know how to make your dreams materialize. You are both imaginative and creative but in different ways. Your partner has a unique, somewhat offbeat originality and is comfortable living with some chaos—they actually thrive on it, and it enhances their creativity. You are gifted in combining colors and materials; you could be an interior designer, architect, or fashion designer.

If there is an area that could cause friction, it is that both of you are quite opinionated. You tend to be politically minded, an idealist, and someone easily affected by perceived injustice, whereas your partner prefers not to take politics too seriously. This potential stress point is likely to affect you more than your partner, and you would do well to back off when you feel your frustration rise. Your partner may appear happy-go-lucky and perhaps even superficial at times, but make no mistake, they know what they want and will not allow you, or anyone else for that matter, to interfere.

Your partner is a 4

This is not an easy combination, and making this relationship work in the long run will take some effort. On the upside, if it does work, it will be because there is a good balance between freedom and commitment.

The 9 Life Path and the 4 Life Path don't have much in common and tend to have very different attitudes toward life and its many challenges and opportunities.

You are an idealist with little or no prejudice toward people, regardless of culture, race, or religion. In fact, you love to be introduced to people with entirely different histories and backgrounds. Your partner is grounded and secure in their world and generally not particularly interested in other cultures. They like to travel, but they prefer an organized and predictable tour, whereas you are willing to just hop on a plane and go as far as possible. This difference between you and your partner is reflected in other areas of life too. Whether you are buying a house or discussing a new venture, you will almost have different, if not opposing, desires and expectations.

It is likely that a powerful physical attraction was the catalyst that started your relationship, and maintaining and appreciating that will greatly help you overcome other obstacles, but it may not be enough. Most important, you need to give each other freedom and plenty of opportunity to go your own way. This is not estrangement but a way to value and grow what binds you while creating distance from the things that may become problematic in your relationship.

You are very different in many ways, and you need to recognize and accept that. For this relationship to be lasting and satisfactory, trust is key. Your partner may have more of a tendency to be jealous or possessive, but bear in mind, this is due to a fear of losing you. Be generous in expressing your love, physically and verbally; tell them you love them often and sincerely—this may be your most powerful tool to overcome the obstacles, and they will be less likely to become jealous. Your partner needs solid ground under their feet, in career and in romance. Without that, they feel vulnerable.

You too need to know your partner has your back, even if, compared to most couples, you maintain a bit of distance. Love, by definition, is invisible. Only reflections of love can be seen and felt, and that is what you both need.

Your partner is a 5

It's quite surprising and uncommon that you are in a romantic relationship, especially if you've been in it for several years. This means that you have overcome many obstacles, and your relationship is strong and based on a powerful connection. Your Life Path number tells us that you are more subdued, deliberate, and idealistic. Your partner's Life Path is 5, which means they are sociable, outgoing, energetic, adventurous, and thrive on change and a bit of chaos.

Your partner is more sensual and enjoys expressing their love for you generously, through physical touch as well as verbally. You are less inclined to reach out. You just don't like to display your affection except in privacy and special moments, but that doesn't mean your love is less strong or committed. This may be frustrating for your partner, as you can seem distant and aloof at times. You would do well to let your partner know that you love them as often as you can. It will certainly strengthen the relationship and make your partner feel more secure and included in your inner life.

Although you have different likes and dislikes, one commonality between you is that you both love to travel. However, you have different reasons for traveling. You want to explore different cultures and learn from the people who live there. You want to improve their lives and would like to be involved in something that makes you feel that you are part of the solution. Your partner is more motivated by a strong need for freedom and adventure. Still, you should be able to share a lot of experiences while traveling.

Other aspects of your personalities have the potential to be strongly connected and compatible. Both of you can adapt to changes and are willing to compromise, although your partner is more flexible than you and actually embraces change. You are likely more conservative and careful in making life choices or forcing changes.

It's essential to recognize and accept each other's differences to avoid unnecessary conflicts. You should understand that excessive idealism and self-righteousness may not impress your partner and perhaps even become a source of irritation. Your partner is all in favor of helping people, but they tend to distrust entirely altruistic motivations. Your partner may also feel you sometimes appear hard to reach and not very interested in what's going on with them. It will improve your relationship if you make a conscious effort to show interest in their endeavors, but you must walk a fine line. Your partner is very independent and cannot stand being limited or told what to do, so your interest should not include intruding on their territory.

There may be times you feel your partner is shallow or selfish when they are not as driven to change the world as you are. You feel depth and idealism should be part of everyone's makeup, and may, at times, indulge in self-righteousness and appear condescending to others.

There are also areas where you complement and learn from each other. Your partner's love for freedom and excitement can inspire you to step outside your comfort zone and try new things, while your innate sense of empathy, compassion, and spirituality can balance out your partner's more impulsive and reckless tendencies.

Overall, the compatibility between Life Path number 9 and Life Path number 5 depends on the individuals' willingness to embrace each other's differences and find ways to support each other.

Your partner is a 6

This is one of the best possible combinations. Your Life Path number 9 is associated with humanitarianism, spirituality, and compassion, while your partner's Life Path number 6 is associated with love, family, and service. The difference is that in your case, you are focused on the world at large, while your partner is more concerned with the people close to them. When it comes to compatibility between these two Life Path numbers, there is potential for a strong and fulfilling partnership, as they share many similarities in their approach to life.

Life Path 9 and Life Path 6 can complement each other well in a romantic relationship, as they both have a strong desire to serve others and make a positive impact on the world. Your idealistic, spiritual, and humanitarian focus can inspire and motivate others. Similarly, your partner's nurturing and caring nature provides a sense of stability and emotional support for others. As you can see, both you and your partner tend to have a supportive and positive influence on those around you, as well as on each other.

However, there may also be some areas of tension. Your partner can be overly focused on the needs of others and may neglect their own needs, which can be frustrating for you, and make you feel that you are not receiving enough attention or support. Similarly, you can become so involved with humanitarian, political, or spiritual causes that you become distant and out of reach; at least, your partner may feel that way. There is a distinct danger of gradually moving in different directions and losing touch with your partner without realizing that it's happening—a slow path to estrangement without any actual fights or discordance. The way to overcome this is by reaching out regularly and being interested in each other's endeavors.

Overall, the compatibility between Life Path number 9 and Life Path number 6 depends on the individuals involved and their willingness to communicate openly and support each other's needs. With effort and understanding, they can build a strong and fulfilling relationship based on mutual respect and a shared desire to serve others.

In addition, you are both creative, you both love design and other forms of visual art. However, you are also both quite opinionated in these matters and that can cause clashes. It is important to recognize this and compromise in such circumstances. As a rule of thumb, the 9 and 6 make wonderful romantic and friendship relationships, but don't always work well together, unless it is in the areas of healing and teaching. In the world of design and art, you are likely to have a less compatible business relationship. On the other hand, both the 9 and the 6 have a strong sense of justice and are often involved in political or humanitarian causes—areas where you work very well together.

A word of caution: you may have to guard against becoming arrogant and self-righteous—it is a common pitfall for a 9 Life Path. Your partner's weak side is a tendency to let anger and other negative emotions fester until they rear their ugly heads, often entirely unexpected to you. You will wonder what happened for your partner to suddenly display such anger, but you should know that the anger is directly proportionate to their love—so communicate; sit down, hold hands, and talk about what is bothering them. This combination is one of the most compatible, but it is not without vulnerability. If you can communicate, you will be fine, and your relationship has the potential to be loving and long-lasting.

Your partner is a 7

This is a rare combination, not only in a romantic relationship, but any other kind of relationship as well. You don't see many friendships or even business partnerships between a person with a 9 Life Path and a 7 Life Path.

Although you are compatible in some areas, you probably don't share many interests.

A 7 Life Path and a 9 Life Path usually get along well, if there isn't too much interaction—both of you need private space and tend to be a little distant compared to most people. However, the way you maintain that distance is very different. Your partner has an active internal life, they're introspective and more an observer than an active part of a social event, and they are a seeker and thinker while you can be somewhat aloof and may even seem somewhat arrogant because of a sense of separation.

Another potential incompatibility is that you can sometimes be emotionally intense and may struggle to understand your partner's more detached and cerebral approach to life. Your partner, on the other hand, can become overly analytical and have difficulty relating to your more emotional and compassionate nature.

Life Path 9 and Life Path 7 both have a deep interest in spirituality and personal growth but in different and not particularly compatible ways. You are focused on serving others and making a positive impact on the world, which is the way you express your spiritual side, while your partner is less inclined to be a volunteer or devote time and energy to bettering the world. They value intellectual pursuits and introspection and view their spirituality as a very private and internal experience that does not require action to be expressed. This difference in spirituality and personal growth can become an area of discontent and discord, especially because you view the lack of action and involvement in the betterment of mankind as a weakness and a shortcoming.

Every number combination has challenges. Yours will likely revolve around differing interests and your contrasting views on issues that arise. However, you have a need for some distance even between you and your romantic partner, and your partner feels the same way—this satisfies an important need for both of you and can be the basis of a long and loving relationship.

Your partner is an 8

This can be a dynamic and successful pairing, as both numbers are associated with power, ambition, and leadership, albeit in very different ways. There are also some potential challenges that may arise in this relationship.

The contrast between your Life Path 9 and your partner's Life Path 8 can be a source of growth and enrichment. While you may not share the same life goals, your differences can complement each other. Your partner's ambition and determination can inspire you to achieve your humanitarian aspirations on a grand scale, while your compassion and altruism can remind your partner of the deeper meaning and purpose in their pursuits.

Life Path 8 individuals are often driven by a desire for success and material wealth. They are natural leaders and tend to be skilled at managing resources and taking calculated risks. They are also determined and resilient and can overcome obstacles with relative ease.

Life Path number 9 individuals, on the other hand, are more focused on humanitarian and social causes. They are compassionate and empathetic and have a strong sense of justice and fairness. They are often driven by a desire to help others and make the world a better place.

When these two numbers come together in a relationship, there can be a lot of mutual respect and admiration. The number 8 can provide the drive and ambition needed to achieve success and material wealth, while the number 9 brings a sense of purpose and social responsibility to the relationship.

However, there may also be some challenges to overcome. Your partner can sometimes be overly materialistic or status-driven, which may clash with your idealistic and humanitarian tendencies, while you can be too self-sacrificing or emotionally intense, which may be overwhelming and rather disturbing to your partner's more practical and grounded nature.

The key to a successful relationship lies in finding a balance between your individual paths and appreciating the unique qualities each of you brings to the table. By recognizing the strength in your diversity and nurturing a profound respect for one another's values, you can build a lasting and fulfilling partnership that thrives on the synergy of your contrasting Life Paths.

Your partner is a 9

This combination often creates a partnership that goes well beyond romance. Both idealists, you are sufficiently focused and have enough clarity of purpose to devote your life to a single goal, paying little or no attention to the monetary aspects. Contrary to what one might expect, this often results in financial prosperity, although usually not until somewhat later in life.

Most likely, the recognition of your similar outlooks was the reason for the initial attraction between you. Mutually inspiring endless conversations likely helped you feel your dreams were attainable and something you could pursue together. Your bond is strong and should not weaken over time since you thrive on sharing each other's experiences. Your compatibility is powerful and strengthens each of you as individuals. You may find yourselves choosing similar careers, perhaps even within the same organization or institution. These similarities make others see you as an unbreakable couple.

However, some areas of potential discord still exist, even in this extremely compatible combination. The number 9 shows a tendency to believe in concepts and ideals to such an extent that it becomes an obsession. Self-righteousness, narrow-minded thinking, and religious fanaticism are not uncommon, nor are arrogance, pride, and superficial confidence. This helps explain the fact that the 9 is often found among political and religious extremists. Excessive belief in your ideals could also cause problems in your relationship if your concepts differ or your partner feels that you devote too much time to an organization or a venture, especially if your partner does not support it. It is important for both of you to remain open to the ideas of others outside your relationship, and even your family, to respect differing opinions, and to remain humble.

The greatest danger in a relationship between two people with a 9 Life Path appears when one or both of you loses the ability for honest self-criticism and self-examination. It is essential to keep in mind that even with idealism, *moderation* is required—in fact, it is the key word for safeguarding this otherwise promising combination.

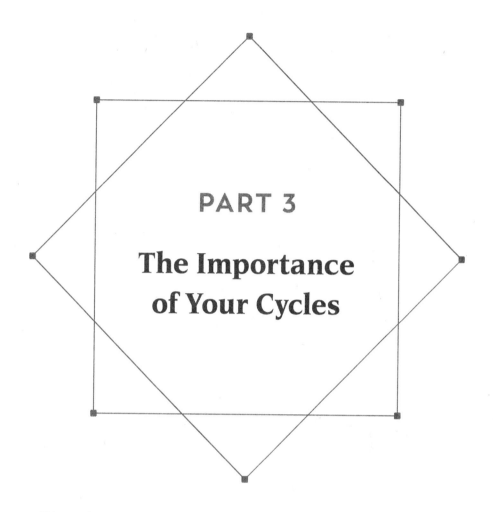

PART 3

The Importance of Your Cycles

Everywhere we look in nature, we see cycles—some long-term, some short-term, and sometimes we can even recognize cycles within cycles. It is no different for people. There are a range of cycles we experience. As I mentioned earlier, even your life can be seen as a cycle, a cycle that is represented in your Life Path number. But there are many other cycles, some as long as nine or twenty-seven years, others lasting one year. However, the cycles that are most strongly felt within relationship compatibility are your Personal Month cycles. Because they are relatively short and intensely felt, they can wreak havoc on your relationship, bring healing or rebirth, and anything in between.

In the next part of the book, you will learn how to find your monthly numbers for each month and those of your partner and read to what extent they influence your relationship. I recommend that you do this at the beginning of every month, as it will almost certainly have a beneficial effect on your relationship. After all, the more you know and understand about you and your partner's circumstances, emotional statuses, priorities, and so forth, the more likely it is that you maintain harmony and peace and move toward a better future.

How to find your monthly numbers

There is one number that is central to all your cycles; that is your Sun Number. (You already found it previously when you calculated your Life Path number.) You can find your Sun Number on the intersection of your day and month of birth in the chart on the following page. Make a note of it—your Sun Number is the basis of all your personal cycles.

Your monthly number is connected to the current year and month, so let's find out what that is. No worries, the math is simple.

Add the current year to the current month.

For example, for May, the 5th month of 2024, add $5 + 2024 = 2029$. Then reduce 2029 to a single digit by adding $2 + 0 + 2 + 9 = 13$. Next, add $1 + 3$ for the final single-digit number, 4. The monthly number for our example is 4.

Now just add that 4 to your Sun Number.

If your Sun Number is 2, your monthly number for May would be $2 + 4 = 6$.

Sometimes you may get a double-digit number. If that is the case, simply reduce it to a single digit, using the method you are now familiar with.

Sun Number

MONTH OF BIRTH

DAY OF BIRTH	January and October	February and November	March and December	April	May	June	July	August	September
1, 10, 19, 28	2	3	4	5	6	7	8	9	1
2, 11, 20, 29	3	4	5	6	7	8	9	1	2
3, 12, 21, 30	4	5	6	7	8	9	1	2	3
4, 13, 22, 31	5	6	7	8	9	1	2	3	4
5, 14, 23	6	7	8	9	1	2	3	4	5
6, 15, 24	7	8	9	1	2	3	4	5	6
7, 16, 25	8	9	1	2	3	4	5	6	7
8. 17, 26	9	1	2	3	4	5	6	7	8
9, 18, 27	1	2	3	4	5	6	7	8	9

For those of you who prefer charts, find the number on the intersection of the year and month below, add that to your Sun Number, then reduce if necessary. This is your Personal Month number for the current month.

Personal Month

MONTH

YEAR	January and October	February and November	March and December	April	May	June	July	August	September
2024	9	1	2	3	4	5	6	7	8
2025	1	2	3	4	5	6	7	8	9
2026	2	3	4	5	6	7	8	9	1
2027	3	4	5	6	7	8	9	1	2
2028	4	5	6	7	8	9	1	2	3
2029	5	6	7	8	9	1	2	3	4
2030	6	7	8	9	1	2	3	4	5
2031	7	8	9	1	2	3	4	5	6
2032	8	9	1	2	3	4	5	6	7

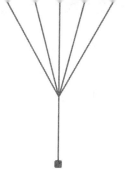

Month Cycle 1

Your partner's monthly number is 1

You share the same cycle number, which is why this will apply to both of you equally. This period promises to be one of new beginnings, new directions, and a greater understanding of yourself and your partner. It is an exciting time full of energy and awakenings to new goals and priorities. It can also bring renewed energy to the relationship, sparking a heightened level of maturity that makes it stronger and more stable.

A temporary disruption is common at the beginning of a new cycle, and the changes you go through will require adjustments to the relationship. Sharing your feelings, doubts, and questions will be more important than ever, so communication is key. Try to devote time to each other, allow for new changes to be absorbed, and be open to your partner's evolving priorities and goals. If you are unable to stay connected and current with your partner's growth, you may end up feeling you have been separated and need to rediscover each other.

This should be a good period for you both, leaving you more confident and capable of handling obstacles and taking advantage of opportunities.

Your partner's monthly number is 2

Although your cycles are entirely different, they should not cause much friction in your relationship.

You are entering a period of renewal, increased energy, and a change of direction in your personal life and career. A 1 cycle enhances your motivation, enthusiasm, and sense of urgency to get things started. As far as you are concerned, nothing moves fast enough. Your partner, on the other hand, is slowing down a bit and is more concerned about feelings and improving their relationship; it is a time when emotions and personal connections are particularly important for them. This could cause them to feel more vulnerable than usual in matters of the heart.

As for career, this is a time for your partner to network, find resources, and align with others, while for you, it is a time to grab the bull by the horns, to take control and get things done; this is dramatically different from your partner's current state of mind. Be aware of that and avoid being critical or overly direct. Unfortunately, this is not easy when you are in a cycle that tends to make you impatient and easily irritated.

If each of you can follow your own path and adjust to your current state of mind without criticism or interference, these cycles tend to support and complement each other. You will be the engine of change and progress while your partner steers and redirects. However, you need to be sensitive and careful not to expect your partner to be as driven as you are at this time. You must also accept that your partner may be a little more demanding than usual. In turn, your partner should avoid making mountains out of molehills or letting emotions override common sense.

Your partner's monthly number is 3

This is one of the most compatible combinations. In fact, your personal numbers ensure future cycles will most likely continue to be relatively harmonious. A gap of two between your numbers will always be maintained, which, as a rule, is a good sign. Your next cycle will be 2 and 4; the period after that will be 3 and 5, and so on.

For this period, you will feel like you woke up refreshed from a long nap and are raring to go. Your energy level is higher than usual; you feel strong, capable, and are not in the mood to be held back by anyone or anything. Your 1 brings dynamic energy and the desire for progress. Your partner also experiences a dynamic, action-driven period, but with less focus and more play. Your partner's energy is directed toward creativity, self-expression, and fun. Although there is work to do, it may not be their top priority.

Generally, the only potential for discord in this combination comes from noticing (and judging) your differences. You might feel your partner is irresponsible, and your partner may feel you should lighten up and have more fun.

On a deeper level, your partner is likely to be a little intimidated by your forceful, go-getter's attitude during this time. To maintain harmony, you will need to recognize that this period represents an important and needed break for your partner, while they must respect your need to stay focused on your goals.

Your partner's monthly number is 4

Although both cycles represent a strong drive and the need to put forth effort, they express it quite differently. You are motivated in large part by enthusiasm, dreams, hope, and a can-do attitude. This is a time of opportunity for you. Take advantage of this period to focus on your goals.

Your partner's drive is born more from frustration and the need to break free from a shell that has felt restrictive for some time. (This frustration is likely to increase before things change.) Your partner's challenge will be to keep from directing it toward you and other loved ones. The 4 cycle is usually not an easy one, but the upside is that it invariably brings progress and a breakthrough of some kind. Both of you should try to keep that in mind as your partner moves through this demanding period.

The two of you are experiencing quite different challenges. You will have to be sensitive to your partner's feelings of frustration and impatience. Your partner feels as if they are slugging through mud with heavy boots and finding obstacles everywhere. They need to stay focused and recognize that they are making progress and that obstacles will be overcome. Still, it is your challenge to weather their impatience and respond by showing support and understanding.

Key words for making this period as harmonious as possible are *patience, understanding,* and *forgiveness*—there will be moments when you lash out at your partner and vice versa, because irritation is right below the surface for both of you.

Make sure you set aside time to share, where the focus is just on enjoying each other's company; go to dinner, invite friends over, or spend a day at the beach. Whatever you can do to get away from the daily grind. You need mini vacations to get you through this cycle.

Your partner's monthly number is 5

This is a somewhat awkward combination; you are at the threshold of a new direction with signs of opportunity and progress everywhere; your partner can also expect a dynamic period, but one when little may go according to plan. If you drew a schematic of these cycles, yours would show a relatively straight line moving in one direction. Conversely, your partner's diagram would show many bends and curves and curling back and forth as if there is no direction at all.

On the upside for your relationship, you both create change and movement, neither one of you feels stagnated, but as you probably guessed, your partner may need support and encouragement to keep them going and help them from getting disillusioned while they are on that roller-coaster ride.

For your partner, the key word is *discipline*; they need to stay focused and yet flexible. For you, the key is to go for it, grab the bull by the horns. Whatever your goals are, take advantage of this cycle's enhanced energy and reach for them. However, with your hands full and your focus single-mindedly on your personal needs and opportunities, you both will probably find less time and opportunity to pay attention to each other, and that would be unfortunate.

It might be helpful to talk about this and put a schedule in place, or an agreed commitment to dedicate time together—perhaps going out or just sitting and talking, to prevent a sense of alienation.

Your partner's monthly number is 6

Your commitment to each other is likely to be tested during this cycle, when outside influences could negatively affect you. The potential turmoil you face could make your relationship feel unstable. As this is one of the most challenging combinations, your greatest strength will be your faith in each other and your ability to trust and rely on each other.

Your 1 cycle will direct your attention outward at a time when your partner's focus is centered on the home front, practical issues, and relationships. Both of you may experience some unfounded jealousy, as the 1 and 6 cycle feel almost as though you are moving in opposite directions and thereby turning your backs on each other.

You will be focused on your goals and may be unaware of signals that alert you to your partner's need for attention. But it is also likely you could become jealous of the attention your partner receives from other people, because a 6 cycle makes a person more approachable and welcoming of attention; if there is anyone in your circle of friends and acquaintances with a romantic eye for your partner, that person will be tempted to express it during this cycle.

Your partner will need to recognize that your dynamic, goal-oriented cycle will distract you from your relationship. Encourage them to let you know if they feel left out. You both will benefit from making a conscious effort to stay connected even if it proves to be inconvenient.

Your partner's monthly number is 7

The challenge for a relationship during these cycles is to maintain a feeling of belonging. There are big differences between the way the 1 and the 7 affect us, but one thing the cycles have in common is that they increase the awareness of independence and individuality. During this period, both of you are likely to feel a little distance in your relationship, which is not necessarily negative.

However, if your expectation is that you will spend a great deal of time together and share everything, and that nothing will change, your expectations may fall short. The wise thing to do is to accept that you will probably move apart somewhat during this period as a temporary and necessary part of your personal growth and, in the long run, the stability and harmony of your relationship.

When you have a 1 in this position, it indicates you will be focused on your career or other goals, busily taking advantage of opportunities for progress. Your partner's attention will be focused inward toward spiritual and mental growth. Your partner is going through a period of self-discovery and needs to spend time alone as part of that process.

Although different in nature, you both have individual needs that require focusing more on yourselves and less on your partner. This may make you feel as if the relationship is weakening. However, unless you turn it into an issue, this should not be the case. If you accept the fact that you are both focused elsewhere, you will find that this period offers growth for you as an individual, but not at the cost of the relationship.

Your partner's monthly number is 8

The combination of 1 and 8 is excellent on the surface but hides some potential pitfalls. On the upside, it will inspire both of you to get busy, to make progress and move toward your goals, but in different ways. You know where you want to go, but your partner is less decisive and may flounder a bit despite their considerable effort.

You are both treading on a path of progress. Yours is straight ahead, and your partner's goals are not so certain but may turn out to be very rewarding. By the end of this cycle, your partner may well stumble onto a promising investment or otherwise experience a financial windfall.

Keep in mind, the gap between these cycles is considerable and has to do with your different spiritual paths—a distinction that may become particularly clear during this period and could create some stress within the relationship. Much of this is likely to be inconsequential (a useful bit of advice is to ignore issues that are not significant). Usually, to maintain a healthy relationship, you need to talk about your differences. However, there are occasions when it is better to avoid touchy subjects and accept that you are individuals with differing opinions and approaches. This is a time to ignore your differences and simply enjoy each other's company.

You both are going through cycles that strengthen your position materially; during this period your best approach is to focus on that. As far as contrasts in your intellectual or spiritual viewpoints, save them for another time.

Your partner's monthly number is 9

Once every nine cycles, your relationship goes through a challenging period, a time when only your love and commitment will see you through. Your current cycle is likely to bring disagreements and arguments that make you wonder what happened to the nice person you used to know. This is due to being at opposite ends of the spectrum. You have a 1 cycle bringing energy, optimism, new ideas, and plans, while your partner is at the tail end of their cycles, which brings completion, finality, and generally makes them feel tired, stressed, and slow. Conflicts can quickly intensify, in part owing to your partner's emotional vulnerability during a period when you may be less sensitive than usual.

There are few, if any, cycle combinations as challenging as this one, but with effort and recognition of your love for each other, your relationship can survive and grow stronger. For you, the most important piece of advice is to give your partner plenty of attention; try to be sensitive to potential mood swings, even if you feel your partner is overly melodramatic.

The advice for your partner is not to take their own emotions too seriously. Your partner is going through changes that require surrender and acceptance, which could make them even more emotional. They will also benefit from realizing that you do not mean to be abrupt or insensitive; you are just in a more energetic and upbeat cycle than they are.

Only your hearts can save the day. When emotions are high, it is often the heart, not the mind, that is able to understand and weather the storm.

CHAPTER 2

Month Cycle 2

Your partner's monthly number is 1

During this time, you may notice that you are slowing down a bit and becoming more focused on your feelings and relationships. Personal connections and emotional intimacy are especially important to you now. However, this may also leave you feeling more vulnerable than usual when it comes to matters of the heart.

Regarding your career, it's a good time to network and seek out resources to help you align with others. On the other hand, your partner may be feeling more ambitious and focused on taking control and getting things done. This is quite different from your current mindset, so it's important that your partner is aware of that and avoids being too critical or direct. However, your partner may be feeling more impatient and easily irritated because of their own cycle, so you may want to give them some slack.

Your partner is entering a period of renewal, increased energy, and a possible change of direction in their personal and/or professional life. Their motivation, enthusiasm, and sense of urgency to get things started are all heightened during this time. However, this can also lead to feelings of frustration, since they may feel like nothing moves fast enough for them.

Ideally, both you and your partner can follow your own paths and adjust to your current state of mind without interfering with or criticizing each other. Your cycles can complement and support each other, with your partner being the engine of change and progress while you steer. However, it's important for your partner to be sensitive and careful not to expect you to be as driven as they are at this time.

You should also be mindful of not making a big deal out of small issues or letting your emotions override common sense. By being aware of each other's cycles and adjusting accordingly, you can navigate this time with greater ease and harmony.

Your partner's monthly number is 2

After the changes you experienced during the last cycle's dynamic energy, you are probably ready for things to slow down a bit, and on the material plane, that will most likely be the case. In addition, this cycle will bring support from others to help you further your goals in all areas of your life, so in many ways, this is a good time for both of you. However, this is also a time when emotions rule, which can cause problems you would prefer to avoid. In other words, your circumstances will almost certainly improve or stabilize, and this will bring some relief, but as far as your relationship goes, you may run into some emotional issues.

The main challenges and changes in this cycle will relate to the deeper aspects of your relationship. This period will find you more vulnerable and sensitive to anything related to the heart. Where a small argument may have made barely a dent during any other time, a similar confrontation could easily become a major issue now. You will need to be particularly sensitive to each other and take advantage of every opportunity to convey your love. With advanced notice that this period could be particularly emotional, you should remind yourselves—and each other—not to let minor irritations fester.

The upside over the course of this cycle is that you will likely find your love for each other to be maturing and growing stronger despite some irrational and emotional episodes earlier during the cycle. But this will be true only if you express your love as well as your need for your partner's attention. The best way to move through this period is to prioritize your relationship without succumbing to extreme emotions.

Your partner's monthly number is 3

When cycles fall next to each other in number sequence (like your 2 and 3), it creates very different needs and experiences for those in a relationship.

Your 2 indicates this will be a cycle when emotions are felt more intensely and have more impact than usual. You might feel like a protective layer has been lost, leaving you vulnerable. During this same period, your partner will experience heightened inspiration, enthusiasm, confidence, and creativity—a lighthearted time when sensitive emotions play a lesser role.

The likelihood that you will be strongly affected by your feelings could lead to mood swings, emotional insecurity, or confusion. Coupled with your partner's upbeat attitude and probably lessened sensitivity and intuition, this could create challenges for your relationship.

There may be occasions when your partner doesn't understand why you are so upset about what they consider a minor argument, and you might wonder why your partner seems so distracted and uncaring.

The best advice for your partner is to be sensitive to your concerns and give you extra time and attention. You can help by not dwelling on your emotions. If your partner seems a bit caught up in other things, it is probably because they feel secure enough in the relationship to focus on the creative endeavors and social events that are an integral part of their current cycle. If you need attention or a more sensitive approach, let them know.

You will both have to make room for your differences. Recognizing you are going through very different cycles can help you better understand and tolerate each other.

Your partner's monthly number is 4

Your cycles carry many similarities and a few differences. This is a time of growth for you, through networking, work relationships, and consolidating plans. Your partner will focus on work; they will need to put forth extra effort and probably will experience a fair amount of frustration.

The focal point for both of you should be your career, projects, plans, and future. Your relationship should not pose much of a challenge, although it may feel as if you don't communicate or share as much time together as usual and perhaps you even sense that you are pulling away from each other. While it is usually important to address relationship concerns promptly, during this project- and career-oriented cycle, you may find there isn't time to devote to other things.

However, this is only one side of the coin. Although you may feel somewhat separated during this period, on a more subtle level you have the potential to form a deeper sense of yourselves and your relationship. Your partner's 4 inspires the need to find stability and comfort. It is a time to place things where they belong and to establish boundaries. The heart rules you, so your emotions are likely to be strongly felt and quickly expressed. These qualities complement each other. While your partner works on the practical side of the relationship, you can help move it to a deeper level.

Your partner's monthly number is 5

The 2 and the 5 get along well in many ways. They happily play together, love together, and enjoy each other's company—if everything is in harmony. However, the moment they hit a bump in the road, things can quickly turn bad and irrational. The trick is to avoid disagreements as much as possible. Although it is not usually recommended, this may be one of those times when it is best to keep things somewhat superficial and not dig too deep.

For you, the enhanced emotional vulnerability typical of a 2 cycle could open the door to negative feelings that are out of proportion with what is really going on. A minor criticism could become a major source of discontent during this period. At the same time, your partner may not be as sensitive and aware as usual, which could lead to impulsive comments that hurt your feelings—restraint and self-control are needed right now.

Your partner experiences a dynamic cycle that will make them feel caught in a whirlwind of changes and opportunities. As with the relationship itself, when things are harmonious, it all feels good and manageable, but it's like driving a fast car: not paying attention for one moment can cause a problem. Your partner may therefore not pay as much attention to your needs as you would like, and it is up to you to accept that and not misread it as a lack of interest and caring.

You are in calmer waters and should play a supportive role; be tactful and give your partner enough room to feel free to respond to whatever changes life is throwing at them. A sense of freedom is an absolute must for your partner during this cycle.

Your key words for this period are *commitment* and *honesty*, along with taking each other's emotions seriously. You should try not to exaggerate them, and your partner should guard against patronizing you.

Your partner's monthly number is 6

This combination can create either a highly positive environment or a decidedly negative one, as both cycles, the 2 and the 6, are emotionally charged and sensitive, albeit in different ways. You might find yourself emotionally on edge, often without clear reason. Disagreements are likely, but how you handle them is critical. You are particularly sensitive, and if your partner isn't careful with their words, you may feel hurt or offended without real cause.

Your partner may not always get it right, but they are driven by the heart during their 6 cycle, so it's beneficial to give them the benefit of the doubt. For both of you, hidden or suppressed emotional issues may surface, often triggered by minor incidents, and you might blow them out of proportion. It's important to recognize when you might be making mountains out of molehills.

Influenced by the 6 cycle, your partner will be driven by emotions differently. They are likely to address problems with generous displays of affection, as the 6 cycle is passionate and loving. This might be just what you need, unless your partner overlooks the root causes of your distress. Everyone wants to feel understood, even if their concerns seem minor. If emotions clash and logic is absent, the outcome can be harmful.

Your key words for this cycle are *forgiveness* and *tolerance*.

Your partner's monthly number is 7

Your individual cycles do not have much in common during this period, but they shouldn't produce many relationship challenges.

Although your 2 cycle could heighten your sensitivity, you should try not to attach too much importance to your emotional ups and downs. This period is best spent on practical matters and determining what is most important to you.

During this period, it might feel like your partner is distant at times and lives in a world that excludes you. In a way, this is true. Your partner experiences a period of self-reflection, concerned with the inner mysteries of life from a philosophical, intellectual, or spiritual perspective. Your best response is to focus on your own life—especially the practical side, your career, home, finances, and so forth.

If either of you feels your partner is more interested in their needs than in those of the relationship, consider that this is not necessarily negative or selfish, nor is it an indication the relationship is in trouble. Your needs and priorities are just different right now; the relationship should be quite safe since neither of you has a desire to rock the boat. Allowing each other the space and freedom to pursue individual interests can ultimately strengthen your relationship.

Your partner's monthly number is 8

This is considered a difficult combination of cycles because your priorities are not aligned. For you, relationships and matters of the heart take precedence and heighten your sensitivity and emotions. This could make you more vulnerable to criticism or perceived neglect.

For your partner, focusing on the relationship will probably take second or third place for a while. Their focus will be on career, finances, friends, and family. Your partner wants to improve everything that surrounds and sustains the relationship, but in the process, they may not pay as much attention to you. Also, they might feel you aren't carrying enough emotional weight when, in fact, your focus is simply directed elsewhere.

This cycle combination offers many openings for misunderstanding and disagreement. It is likely that you will experience a few rough spots, but it should also bring positive aspects. Your partner has the potential to make improvements in areas outside the relationship, which will ultimately support it, while you can help the two of you stay connected and deepen your bond on the emotional plane.

Your partner's monthly number is 9

This cycle may help you determine if your relationship is founded on real substance. Although your experiences will differ, your numbers indicate you are both facing a period when emotions rule.

You may be somewhat self-absorbed and emotional about pretty much everything. Vulnerable and sensitive, you will also be more finely tuned and able to recognize what is real and what is not. For the heart to see clearly, protective layers need to be removed, which may leave you feeling more exposed than usual.

For your partner, a different but no less emotionally charged period is reflected in their 9. They are also searching for answers, but their questions are less concerned with the relationship than they are about choosing the best path to take as they approach a crossroad. Although this is a very important cycle for your partner—a time of growth and choice—it is also likely to be a period with many ups and downs.

As you work through your individual issues during this cycle, you may find you are able to support each other in only the most basic sense: you can reassure each other of your love.

If the relationship has real substance, you will move through this time with flying colors. If it does not, you will still have a better understanding of the way your relationship will weather periods when your individual needs and objectives are different.

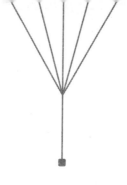

CHAPTER 3

Month Cycle 3

Your partner's monthly number is 1

As a rule of thumb, the most harmonious combination of numbers is when there is a gap of two, as in 3 and 1. And because the cycles follow a consistent rhythm, you will always have a gap of two. That said, the happy-go-lucky, creative, and optimistic influence this cycle offers you goes well with your partner's current cycle, even though they are considerably more focused and driven at this time. In fact, you might feel your partner is a little too forceful, to the point it can make you uncomfortable, but you can counter that with your more relaxed and playful approach.

You are in a mental and emotional upswing. However, there can be residue from past cycles that still linger. The second half of this cycle will be more uplifting and joyful than the first part.

Your partner is at the start of something new, both on the material plane and on the mental and emotional planes. They are invigorated and ready to take charge. You may have to just step aside and let them go for it. You don't want to get in their way. Offer support and encouragement, not caution or hindrance. It is up to them to recognize what is possible and what isn't.

You also experience a dynamic period, but with less focus and more play. As a result, your partner may complain that you are wasting your time and your energy. Explain to them that to find a way forward, we sometimes need to walk some dead-end streets—it's not wasting time, it's finding the right way.

Your partner's monthly number is 2

When cycles align in sequential numbers, such as your 3 and 2, it brings forth distinct needs and experiences for both individuals in a relationship.

Your partner's 2 cycle indicates a time of heightened emotions, where feelings are experienced more intensely and carry greater impact than usual. They may sense a loss of a protective layer, leaving them vulnerable. Conversely, during this same period, you will experience a surge of inspiration, enthusiasm, confidence, and creativity. It is a light-hearted phase where sensitive emotions take a back seat.

The intensity of your partner's emotions and their susceptibility to mood swings, emotional insecurity, or confusion may be prominent. Coupled with your upbeat attitude, which may reduce your sensitivity and intuition, these differences can pose challenges for your relationship.

There might be instances when you struggle to comprehend why your partner becomes deeply upset over what you consider a minor disagreement, while your partner may question why you appear distracted and seemingly uncaring. The best course of action for you is to be sensitive to your partner's concerns and offer them additional time and attention during this cycle. On the other hand, they can assist by not dwelling excessively on their emotions. If you appear preoccupied with other matters, it is because you feel secure enough in the relationship to focus on creative endeavors and social engagements, which are integral to your current cycle. If your partner requires attention or a more delicate approach, they should openly communicate their needs.

Both of you must create space for your differences and acknowledge that you are going through contrasting cycles. This awareness can foster a deeper understanding between you.

Your partner's monthly number is 3

This should be a period where you can enjoy each other's company, share ideas, and experience relatively little stress in most areas of your life. The key word is *relative*. The 3 you share during this cycle suggests most things should be easier to handle and problems will not weigh on you as much as they might at another time. However, there is always another side to the coin. The 3 can also make you a little unfocused and scattered—a typical side effect of its creative nature. If you have set specific goals, you may find your ability to stay centered and disciplined more challenging than usual.

Your relationship has the potential to strengthen and deepen during this time. You connect easily and your ability to communicate will be enhanced. The only drawback may be your heightened popularity. The charismatic energy of this cycle will likely attract attention from other people. This attention could be tempting to either or both of you, giving rise to jealousy. If you feel negative emotions because of other people paying more attention to your partner, remember your partner is probably feeling the same way. Talk about it, and have a laugh—you can afford it, because your relationship is not weakened but strengthened by this; after all, who doesn't feel a little pride when they witness their partner's popularity?

Your partner's monthly number is 4

During this period, your cycles will be pushing you in opposite directions. Your numbers, 3 and 4, suggest this is probably often the case in your relationship—but it does not necessarily reflect incompatibility.

For you, this is a time to relax and smell the roses, while your partner needs to stay focused and maintain a high level of effort. It is important that you don't try to change each other's inclination to follow the demands of your individual cycles. Your partner needs to accept the fact that you are not as disciplined and ambitious as usual, while you should guard against trying to talk your partner into taking it easy and not being so uptight.

Contrary to what one might expect, as a rule, cycles with a gap of one (like your 3 and 4) are not always incompatible even though they move in different directions. In fact, they often complement each other. Their differences normally cause stress only if couples try too hard to influence each other.

You should be allowed to back off a little from the daily grind, and your partner will need support and encouragement during what could be a rather demanding cycle.

Your partner's monthly number is 5

This is one of the most compatible cycle combinations. You both have numbers that deliver enhanced energy and dynamic growth.

This is a period to play off your partner's energy and enjoy each other's company. Your ability to communicate should also be enhanced. This is considered a healing cycle, because it is known to impart less stress and more flexibility to the body and the mind.

There is little negative to say about your combination other than the inherent danger of having too much fun. Quite often the 3 (and especially the 5) invite elements of risk into their search for the new and exciting. Focus and discipline could be concerns as well. Make sure to remind each other to slow down if things begin to get out of balance, and be careful not to attract people whose influence is less than desirable.

Your partner's monthly number is 6

This is a time of strong emotions for both of you. Although inspired by different motives, your numbers suggest you will appreciate each other even more than usual.

For you, this is partly the result of the 3 lending a deeper appreciation of your family, friends, and social life. For your partner, the driving force is simply the heart. Both of you should feel your priorities shift somewhat toward the joy of living and away from the daily grind.

A potential concern during this cycle could lie in your partner's greater need for attention at times when you are focused on your social life and your creative energies, thereby not needing as much attention from them. You may want to remind yourself to pay attention to their emotional needs.

Your partner's monthly number is 7

The 3 and 7 bring together two very different cycles. Your numbers are opposites in the influences they deliver.

Things should lighten up for you like the sun breaking through after days of overcast skies. Your partner's 7 indicates they will experience a period of self-awareness, contemplation, and self-discovery. It is an inward-focused, quiet time for them, while for you, it is the exact opposite;

you are more social and playful, even a bit scattered, and not particularly in a quiet mood.

These differing moods could make communication difficult, which might be frustrating. Your lighthearted, playful disposition may have trouble relating to your partner's pensive and perhaps even pessimistic outlook, while they may have trouble relating to your sunny, upbeat state of mind. To offset this concern, do your best to acknowledge and respond to each other's concerns. Express your love, reach out, and give each other room to explore individual interests.

You will need to understand that the quiet, introverted mood affecting your partner is temporary and necessary. And they should try not to be irritated by your attitude, which may appear superficial to them.

This cycle combination can have a negative effect on relationships. If you feel that you are approaching a danger zone, share your feelings as promptly and honestly as possible. Although you will both be affected by your individual cycles, your partner is likely to be more strongly impacted.

Do your best to support each other during this period. And remember, cycles are temporary by nature. *Patience* and *tolerance* are the key words for both of you.

Your partner's monthly number is 8

Although they are quite different, your cycles are compatible. Creativity, optimism, and inspiration are the main ingredients in your cycle, while the components ruling your partner's cycle are ambition, goals, and financial reward. These influences complement and inspire each other, which should benefit your relationship as well as the more mundane and pragmatic affairs.

This is a favorable time to take care of long-postponed projects such as financial concerns, home repairs, and other practical matters. It is also one of the best combinations for relationships. You will find you re-late and communicate well, and easily support each other's endeavors.

There is, however, an area that could cause discord. Your 3 should help you feel inspired and active, but you will be less focused and disci-plined than usual. This comes at a time when your partner is fully fo-cused, especially on the bottom line. As a result, your partner may feel you are somewhat irresponsible, and you might feel your partner is all work and no play.

Compromise and recognition of the differing aspects of your cycles can help you better understand your partner and allow both of you to capitalize on what this period offers.

Your partner's monthly number is 9

This combination of cycles is quite compatible and often gives birth to new ideas and plans. It should be a time of enhanced creativity for both of you, delivering opportunities for change and improvement. Your part-ner, however, could also face a challenging period of powerful emotions that requires a stable environment and support from you. Fortunately, your cycle is upbeat and optimistic, which can be a much-needed source of comfort for your partner.

Because you will experience differences in your approaches and at-titudes, it is important to respect each other's needs during this cycle. You can help by exercising patience if your partner is not as grounded as usual. They are likely to be experiencing a time of choices and decisions on a deep, even subconscious level, so little may seem clear or simple to them.

You, on the other hand, should have an upbeat, happy-go-lucky ap-proach to life during this cycle, and an easier, less emotional time. There will be ups and downs, but your challenge is more about maintaining direction and focus. Although this may not seem like an ideal time to make big changes, the process of making plans together could help your partner feel more secure.

During this period, much will depend on your ability to be a source of strength and comfort to your partner. Their 9 cycle is considered the most challenging, while yours is usually one of the easiest and most pleasurable. This is a fortunate combination for the relationship—you can share your upbeat energy with your partner and offset their more challenging cycle.

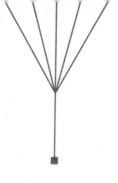

CHAPTER 4

Month Cycle 4

Your partner's monthly number is 1

In general, the combination of 1 and 4 is not a match made in heaven. While both cycles embody a strong drive and the need for exertion, your partner expresses it in a distinct manner; they are fueled by enthusiasm, dreams, hope, and an unwavering can-do attitude. This is their moment of opportunity, and they should seize it to concentrate on their goals.

Conversely, your drive is fueled by frustration and the urge to break free from a confining shell that has restricted you for quite some time. Unfortunately, this frustration is likely to intensify before circumstances change. But take solace in the fact that change will come. Your challenge lies in refraining from venting your irritation onto your partner and loved ones. The 4 cycle is typically arduous, yet it also brings forth progress and a breakthrough of some kind. Both of you should bear this in mind as you tread through this demanding period.

The two of you are confronting divergent challenges. Your partner must tread delicately, being attuned to your feelings of frustration and impatience. It may feel as though you're slogging through mud, encountering obstacles at every turn. Maintain your focus and acknowledge that progress is being made, and hurdles can be surmounted. Meanwhile, it is your partner's trial to weather your impatience and respond with unwavering support and understanding.

Patience, understanding, and forgiveness are the cornerstones of harmonizing this phase as smoothly as possible. There will undoubtedly be moments when both of you inadvertently unleash your frustrations, for the embers of irritation smolder beneath the surface for both parties. It is crucial to set aside dedicated time for enjoying each other's company. Engage in shared experiences such as dining out, inviting friends over, or relishing a day at the beach. Any means of escaping the monotonous routine will suffice. These brief respites will serve as mini vacations, providing the fortitude necessary to navigate through this cycle.

Your partner's monthly number is 2

Your cycles share both similarities and a few distinctions, shaping your experiences in this phase of growth. For your partner, it's a period of expansion through networking, work relationships, and solidifying plans. On the other hand, you are urged to direct your energy toward work, investing extra effort, and preparing for potential frustration. The 4 cycle, although characterized by a sense of sluggishness and increased difficulty, also brings stability and gradual progress.

The focal point for both of you should be your careers, projects, plans, and future aspirations. While your relationship may not present significant challenges, you might notice a decrease in communication and shared time together, and perhaps a sense of drifting apart. Although addressing relationship concerns in a timely manner is typically crucial, during this career-focused cycle, it may be better to focus on other aspects.

However, there is another side to this coin. Amidst the perceived separation, you possess the potential for a deeper understanding of yourselves and your relationship at a more subtle level. Your 4 cycle encourages the establishment of stability and boundaries, seeking comfort and balance. Conversely, your partner's heart governs their emotions, which are likely to be intensely experienced and readily expressed. These qualities complement each other; while you concentrate on the practical aspects of the relationship, your partner can contribute to its growth, pushing it to a more profound level.

Your partner's monthly number is 3

During this period, your cycles will be pulling you in opposite directions. However, this is a common occurrence in your relationship and doesn't necessarily indicate incompatibility.

For your partner, this is a time to embrace relaxation and enjoy the simple pleasures of life. They may prioritize leisure and taking things easy, while you are required to maintain focus and exert a high level of effort. It is crucial to honor each other's natural inclinations driven by your individual cycles. Recognize that your partner may not exhibit their usual level of discipline and ambition, and it's important for you to avoid persuading them to adopt your intense approach.

Contrary to expectations, cycles with a one-point gap (such as your 4 and 3) are not inherently incompatible, as they often complement each other. Any potential stress arises only when couples attempt to exert excessive influence on each other.

Grant your partner the space to step back from the demands of daily life, and, in turn, you will benefit from their support and encouragement during what is likely a challenging cycle for you.

Your partner's monthly number is 4

You share the same cycle number. Since these cycles follow each other in a repeating sequence, you will always share the same personal cycle numbers, and consequently the same influences.

This is a time to focus on strengthening the foundation of your lives. Your career, financial affairs, home, and other practical aspects will take high priority. While this cycle often represents progress, it can be demanding and frustrating; things may not move quickly enough or in accordance with your expectations. Your frustration, coupled with a demanding schedule, could create problems for your relationship.

Since you will always share the same cycles, you are likely to find yourself on parallel tracks. This usually makes your cycles compatible and helps you see eye to eye when it comes to priorities and goals. However, it also means you both could feel frustrated at the same time (during this cycle, for example), which might compound your irritation. When this happens, it is more likely that an outside influence rather than your partner is causing the annoyance. Keeping this in mind can help you step back, talk about your feelings, and discuss solutions instead of fostering negativity.

Your partner's monthly number is 5

This is a period where your individual cycles and influences will be very different. You experience a period of focus, effort, and possibly frustration or stagnation, while your partner goes through a time of change, excitement, and dynamic energy.

Considering that, your partner can help you move forward and not become too frustrated by the demands of your cycle, and you can return the favor by functioning as a rock of stability for them during their more unpredictable and chaotic cycle.

The most positive effect of this combination is that their joint forces almost always deliver progress and decisiveness. By the end of this period, it is likely you will have established new goals and gained more clarity about your future.

A potential negative effect is that, at times, you might move in such different directions you could begin to feel like strangers. This can be avoided by regularly sharing your feelings and ideas. Physical closeness and shared activities will help you stay connected.

Your partner's monthly number is 6

This cycle combination offers several opportunities for you to improve many aspects of your life. Your traits and influences complement each other very well. This is a time of shared effort. You will be focusing on the practical aspects and your partner's focus is on the heart and health of the relationship. Your energies are aligned, which enhances the positive qualities found in the 4 and the 6.

This cycle has the potential to deliver progress, financial growth, and more involvement in your community. It is a good time to combine forces to reach a common goal. Normally, very few negative influences appear with this combination. Even a tendency for you to become irritated or angry more quickly can be lessened by your partner's ability to comfort you. And you can bring a different kind of comfort—that of stability and security—as your focus is very much on improving the material aspects of life.

Your partner's monthly number is 7

This combination has the potential to create distance between you, not because you suddenly have less interest in each other, but because your cycles produce interests and concerns that lead you in different directions.

For you, it is a time to deal with mundane, practical matters, which you could find boring and frustrating. The 7 in your partner's cycle is focused inward—a period for quiet contemplation, daydreaming, doubts, questions, and learning more about who they are. It's not difficult to see how the differing needs inherent in your cycles might create some distance.

Sharing your feelings and giving each other room to pursue individual interests can help alleviate stress in your relationship, and help you take advantage of the progress this cycle has to offer.

Your partner's monthly number is 8

This cycle's combination can be either very positive or quite negative. There is usually no middle ground. You may feel like you are slogging through mud in heavy boots—there is progress, but it probably feels excruciatingly slow and requires considerable effort.

Your partner's experience should be just the opposite, where it feels as if everything is there for the taking. In a relationship, this combination can bring out the best in each of you or enhance your negative traits. For example, your partner's optimistic, ambitious attitude could either be irritating to you or help to alleviate periods of frustration and anxiety. And your effort and methodical approach could be an inspiring influence on them or put a damper on their dynamic energy.

To top it off, it is likely you will both be able to clearly recognize the effect you have on each other during this period. As a result, you will feel either love and appreciation or irritation and blame, depending on the way you respond to each other.

The key to getting the most out of this cycle is to be sensitive to your partner's needs and state of mind. Try not to get so caught up in your own world that you lose touch with theirs.

Your partner's monthly number is 9

The 4 and the 9 are not the most compatible cycles, often causing emotional turmoil in a relationship. This is due, in part, to your partner being at the end of the cycle and a bit worn out, which can make emotions unpredictable. Your partner's 9 will ask them to let go of the old and prepare for the new, which invariably evokes powerful feelings. Your 4, on the other hand, will focus on practical matters that may leave little room for empathy. You will be concerned with career, projects, details, effort, discipline, and tangible progress.

Your partner needs understanding and a sense that you share common goals. You will probably wish your partner would get on with the more practical and immediate business at hand. It is important for both of you to recognize you are going through very different stages. During this cycle, you should stay as close to each other as possible. Make the effort to focus more on your partner and less on yourself and get away from your daily routines to do things you enjoy together.

CHAPTER 5

Month Cycle 5

Your partner's monthly number is 1

This pairing is undeniably peculiar; your partner stands at the threshold of a promising new path, where opportunities and progress abound. Meanwhile, your journey takes on a dynamic nature, characterized by unexpected twists and turns, seemingly lacking a clear trajectory. If we were to depict these cycles graphically, your partner's chart would showcase a steady linear progression, while yours would resemble a convoluted web, looping back and forth without a defined direction.

There is a silver lining when it comes to your relationship. Both of you embody change and motion, ensuring that neither stagnation nor complacency creep into your lives. As you may anticipate, though, you might require support and encouragement to prevent yourself from losing your bearings and succumbing to disillusionment during this exhilarating roller-coaster ride.

Discipline becomes your guiding principle, urging you to remain focused yet adaptable. For your partner, the key lies in seizing the moment, fearlessly grasping opportunities by the horns. Regardless of their aspirations, they should harness the heightened energy of this cycle and relentlessly pursue their goals.

Nevertheless, as your plate becomes filled with personal needs and the pursuit of opportunities, you both might find less time and opportunity to attend to each other. It would be beneficial to have an open conversation about this and establish a schedule or a mutual commitment to dedicating time together. Whether it involves going out on adventures or simply engaging in heartfelt conversations, these intentional acts can help ward off any sense of alienation and strengthen your bond.

Your partner's monthly number is 2

The 2 and the 5 share a harmonious bond in many aspects. They joyfully engage in play, love, and savoring each other's presence, if everything remains in perfect harmony. However, when faced with obstacles, things can swiftly take a turn for the worse.

The key is to steer clear of disagreements as much as possible. While it is not typically advised, this may be one of those times when maintaining a somewhat superficial approach is best.

During a 2 cycle, your partner may be susceptible to heightened emotional vulnerability, which can amplify negative emotions disproportionately. Even a minor criticism can transform into a significant source of discontent during this period. Simultaneously, you may find yourself less sensitive and perceptive than usual, leading to impulsive remarks that may hurt their feelings. The advice for you is to exercise restraint and maintain self-control during this time.

You, on the other hand, are immersed in a dynamic cycle that propels you into a whirlwind of changes and opportunities. Just like the relationship itself, when things are harmonious, everything feels manageable and enjoyable. However, it can be akin to driving a fast car, where a momentary lapse in attention can lead to problems. Consequently, you may not be as attuned to your partner's needs as they would prefer. It is essential for your partner to understand this and not misinterpret it as a lack of interest or care.

Meanwhile, your partner finds themselves in calmer waters and should assume a supportive role, offering tactfulness and providing you with ample space to navigate the changes that life presents. A sense of freedom becomes imperative for you during this cycle.

Your partner's monthly number is 3

This combination of cycles is remarkably harmonious and compatible. Both of you possess numbers that bring heightened energy and facilitate dynamic growth.

During this period, embrace and enjoy the vibrant energy your partner exudes. Take advantage of this time to engage in activities together and savor each other's company. Your communication skills are likely to flourish as well. This cycle is known for its healing qualities, reducing stress, and promoting flexibility in both the body and mind.

There are not many negatives to highlight in your combination, aside from the potential risk of indulging in excessive fun. The nature of the 3, and even more so the 5, often invites a sense of adventure and novelty, which can introduce elements of risk. It's important to maintain a balance and exercise focus and discipline when needed. Remind each other to pace yourselves if things start to become overwhelming, and be cautious not to attract negative influences into your lives.

Your partner's monthly number is 4

During this period, your individual cycles bring forth distinct influences, creating a stark contrast between you and your partner. They are likely to enter a phase of concentration, exertion, and perhaps even frustration or stagnation, while you embark on a journey of change, excitement, and vibrant energy.

Considering these differences, you can assist your partner in moving forward, ensuring they do not succumb to excessive frustration caused by the demands of their cycle. In return, your partner can provide you with a solid foundation of stability during your more unpredictable and tumultuous cycle.

The greatest advantage of this combination is that when your forces align, progress and determination are inevitable. By the conclusion of this period, it is highly likely that you will have set new goals and gained greater clarity about your future path.

However, there is a potential downside to consider. At times, the divergent directions you both take may create a sense of unfamiliarity and detachment, as if you are becoming strangers to each other. This can be mitigated by regularly sharing your feelings and ideas, fostering open communication. Additionally, prioritizing physical closeness and engaging in shared activities will help maintain a strong sense of connection between you.

Your partner's monthly number is 5

This cycle is notorious for creating disorder. Although you are going through the same cycle, you may well experience it very differently, depending largely on your ability to adapt. For those who welcome change and accept it easily, it can translate into a time of excitement, enthusiasm, and promise. Conversely, those who find change and spontaneity difficult could find it a time of anxiety, doubt, or fear. A 5 cycle can bring risks, but it can also be a very enjoyable time if you can "go with the flow."

You might experience this cycle as a period filled with opportunity, while your partner may feel confusion and unpredictability, or vice versa. And it is even quite possible you go back and forth from hope and excitement to fear and doubt. While this is perhaps an exaggeration, it illustrates how two people can experience the same cycle quite differently. In addition, the 5 tends to make you more impulsive and cause you to speak or act before thinking, which could lead to trouble. During this period, it would be easy to project some of the chaos you might experience on a material level onto your partner and others.

Communication is the key to experiencing the best this cycle has to offer. If both of you are ready for new experiences, open to change—and potentially more fun and excitement—this should be an engaging, lively cycle. Just be sure to remind each other that discipline will also be needed to keep things in check.

Your partner's monthly number is 6

Your cycles are as opposite as they can be, yet they are not incompatible. In a relationship, their influences usually complement and balance each other.

You are in a dynamic cycle of change and highly charged, restless energy. Your partner's cycle is one of stability and responsibility, which should make your partner's approach focused and practical. While you are looking for opportunity and adventure, they will be centered on home and family—the people and things that mean the most to them. Your attention will be focused on work, projects, travel, or other outside interests.

If you can recognize the differing aspects of your cycles and support each other's independent paths, this can be a rewarding period for your individual pursuits as well as your relationship. You can inspire a little excitement and they can bring needed stability. There is also the potential for discord, blame, or anger. During this cycle, more than almost any other time, it is important that you do not try to influence each other too much. "Live and let live" should be the slogan for this period.

You have probably already recognized that you always experience very different cycles, some more compatible than others. This is an important aspect of your relationship, and not limited to this cycle. To maintain a successful partnership, you will both need to accept the fact that you will be influenced by very different energies for most of your lives. It wouldn't hurt to make "live and let live" a permanent family slogan.

Although your cycles place you at opposite ends of the spectrum, you complement each other nicely when harmony is maintained, with each of you providing aspects that work well together. Chances are you make a great team when you put your mind to it, especially when it comes to presenting a united front to the outside world.

Your partner's monthly number is 7

This is considered one of the most healing and loving cycles. Although the 5 and the 7 are very different, they get along well.

You are experiencing a time of change and dynamic energy. Your partner will probably be a bit more withdrawn than usual as they focus inward on who they are and where they are going.

Although your cycles tend to influence you very differently—outward focused for you, and inward drawn for your partner—these aspects thrive on one another. Your partner's introspective exploration will probably be attractive to you at a time when you find little that feels subtle or mysterious. And your charged energy and inspiring attitude should have a positive effect on your partner, who may need a connection to the outside world.

It is possible, however, that you could perceive your partner's subdued attitude to mean that something is wrong. Try not to make that mistake. During a 7 cycle, the last thing a person wants is to be drawn out of their contemplative space—and your partner would probably find it annoying and intrusive.

Allow for your differences—just being together is all it takes to make this a wonderful period of closeness and appreciation.

Your partner's monthly number is 8

When it rains, it pours. This is a cycle where neither of you will find it easy to keep up with the other. You will have a lot going on, juggling more balls than usual, while your partner's vision and ambition should keep them focused on plans and opportunities.

With very different energies influencing you during this period, there won't be much room to sit and simply enjoy each other's company. No worries; you should have plenty of time for that during your next cycle when you both shift your focus toward family, friends, and each other.

Your cycle is likely to bring changes, but it will take time (generally several cycles) before you are able to clearly see their full effect. Your energy will probably feel like atoms bouncing everywhere as you explore and establish boundaries. Your partner's cycle will be more focused, which has the potential to put their next goal sharply in focus, centered on a single point.

The most common mistake for couples in this combination is trying to force their perspectives on each other, which could cause frustration and limit this cycle's potential. This is a time when you need to allow each other the freedom to pursue individual objectives without having to explain too much or account for your actions.

Your partner's monthly number is 9

This cycle combination can be quite challenging. It is likely to be a trying time for your partner, who may be uncertain about where to go next. Moreover, there may be few answers for many of your partner's doubts and questions during this period. Their 9 brings the end of a cycle, which could make them feel a little worn out and vulnerable. Fortunately, their next cycle should deliver a much more uplifting, inspiring, and powerful energy.

You should find this to be a period with more energy but less patience than usual. Your 5 delivers dynamic drive and probably a change or two. Your ability to bring excitement and enthusiasm into the relationship could be an excellent tonic for your partner, or, conversely, wear them out and cause irritation.

Both the 5 and 9 cycles are about change, but they are very different in the way we experience them. The changes brought by the 5 tend to be the result of excitement, enthusiasm, and a desire to stir things up. Your partner's 9 cycle has more to do with personal evolution and brings about a completion and cleansing that can be emotionally difficult.

The most important ingredient in making this cycle as beneficial as possible is patience. Your partner will need it during situations that may seem unclear, and you will need it to support them. If things get a bit challenging, keep in mind that although this cycle may not feel particularly compatible, cycles are by definition temporary.

CHAPTER 6

Month Cycle 6

Your partner's monthly number is 1

Your greatest strength during this cycle will be your faith in each other and your ability to trust and rely on each other. This combination is known to be one of the most challenging, and it is likely to put your commitment to the test, especially when external influences begin to negatively impact your partner. The turmoil they face has the potential to make your relationship feel unstable.

In this period, your partner's 1 cycle will direct their attention outward, while your focus centers on practical matters, relationships, and the home front. This juxtaposition may create a sense of moving in opposite directions, leading to unfounded jealousy and a feeling of turning your backs on each other. The combination of the 6 and 1 cycles can be quite tumultuous.

While your partner remains focused on their goals, they may be unaware of signals indicating your need for attention. Simultaneously, there is a possibility that your partner might become jealous of the attention you receive from others. The 6 cycle makes a person more approachable and draws attention, increasing the likelihood of encountering unwanted romantic advances.

It is crucial for you to recognize that your partner's dynamic and goal-oriented cycle may distract them from nurturing your relationship. It's essential to try to communicate if you feel left out and to express your needs. Both of you will benefit from consciously staying connected during this cycle, even if it causes some inconvenience.

Your partner's monthly number is 2

No two cycles are so fully connected to the heart as the 6 and the 2. This is a combination that generally has only two likely outcomes—one quite favorable and the other decidedly not. There is rarely a middle road for this pairing. Fortunately, the influence of these cycles tends to lean toward the favorable.

It is highly likely you will experience major disagreements during this period, and the way you handle them will make all the difference. It will be important for you to respond to each other from your heart rather than taking a rational, analytical approach. You might view this cycle as a spiritual and emotional trial for both of you. Underlying emotional issues often surface under this combination, sometimes during an argument that at first seems superficial.

This cycle should find them mainly focused on their own issues. The 2 tends to amplify emotions, so they may experience anxiety, inner turmoil, or self-doubt, which could make them more needy than usual.

You will also be strongly affected and ruled by the heart, but in a different way; you are more likely to resolve issues by bestowing generous expressions of love—a 6 cycle tends to be sensual and passionate. On one hand, this is just what your partner needs, unless you discount or ignore the reason(s) behind their discomfort. We all want to be taken seriously, even if our reasoning is somewhat superficial.

Your key words for this period are *commitment* and *honesty*, along with taking each other's emotions seriously; your partner should try not to exaggerate them, and you should guard against patronizing them.

Your partner's monthly number is 3

During this period, intense emotions will be experienced by both of you. Interestingly, your respective numbers indicate that you will have an even deeper appreciation for each other than usual, despite being inspired by different motivations.

For your partner, the influence of the number 3 will foster a greater appreciation for family, friends, and social connections. On the other hand, your own driving force stems purely from the heart. As a result, both of you may find your priorities shifting toward embracing the joy of life and stepping away from the monotonous daily routine.

One potential concern that may arise during this cycle is your heightened need for attention, while your partner is primarily focused on their social life and creative pursuits, which may require less attention from you. It's important for your partner to remind themselves to be attentive to your emotional needs, and likewise, you should not hesitate to express your need for attention when you genuinely require it. Open communication is key in navigating this dynamic.

Your partner's monthly number is 4

This combination of cycles presents numerous opportunities to elevate various aspects of your life, with your respective traits and influences synergistically complementing one another.

During this period, a sense of shared effort prevails. Your partner will direct their attention toward practical matters, while you will focus on nurturing the emotional well-being and vitality of the relationship. Your aligned energies magnify the positive qualities inherent in the 6 and 4 cycles.

This cycle holds great potential for progress, financial growth, and deeper engagement within your community. It is an ideal time to join forces and work toward a common goal, leveraging the harmonious blend of your energies.

Typically, very few negative influences arise from this combination. Any tendency for your partner to become easily irritated or prone to anger can be alleviated by your comforting presence. Conversely, they offer a different form of comfort—one rooted in stability and security—as their focus is on enhancing the material aspects of life.

Your partner's monthly number is 5

Your cycles exhibit a fascinating duality that, while distinct from each other, manages to coexist in a relatively balanced manner, adding a unique dimension to your relationship.

Your partner's cycle embodies change and a thirst for adventure and originality, a perpetual pursuit of opportunities in various aspects of life, be it work, projects, travel, or any other external interests that catch their fancy. In stark contrast, your own cycle represents stability and a deep sense of responsibility, anchored firmly in the comforts of home and family. Your priorities revolve around nurturing the people and values that hold the most profound significance in your life.

This inherent contrast is the very essence of what makes your connection so special. Rather than clashing, your diverse cycles act as complementary forces, each bringing something invaluable to the relationship. Your partner's ceaseless energy infuses excitement and dynamism into your life, while your steady, grounded approach provides the essential foundation of stability.

Yet it is essential to acknowledge the potential for friction that this disparity can generate. During these times of divergence, emotions like discord, blame, or even anger may arise. To navigate these challenges successfully, it's crucial to avoid imposing your own rhythms on each other. Embracing a "live and let live" ethos should serve as your guiding principle throughout these contrasting cycles.

It's likely that you've already recognized the recurring pattern of experiencing these divergent cycles in your relationship, and this phase is but one of many. Embracing the influence of these energies is pivotal to sustaining a thriving partnership.

Despite residing at opposite ends of the cycle spectrum, your harmonious coexistence is a testament to the strength of your bond. When you safeguard this harmony, you each have the opportunity to shine in your unique ways. Together, you form an extraordinary team, especially when you present a united front to the world, showcasing the strengths that result from your beautifully intertwined and distinct cycles.

Your partner's monthly number is 6

As a couple, you should have much to offer to each other and those who share your world during this period. Your 6 will find you focused on family, friends, and your relationship. It is a time to share your love and commitment, a time when you easily understand and strengthen each other.

If there is a potential for discord, it would be in taking these loving traits too far. Sometimes caring and nurturing can become intrusive or smothering. It is also possible that one or both of you could become controlling, creating a competitive atmosphere. Another contradiction during these otherwise loving cycles can be lowered tolerance, causing each of you to become irritated more easily over trivial matters.

Although you will probably be more focused on your family, friends, and relationship, practical concerns are favorable as well. This is a good time for finances, promotions, and projects. Material improvement is possible for both of you, although you might also be asked to take on more responsibility.

Your partner's monthly number is 7

You are experiencing very different cycles. On one hand, the influences of 6 and 7 complement each other very well. On the other hand, they create such differing needs that you may find you share little common ground during this period.

The potential exists to disagree on just about everything: how to spend your weekend, what kind of car to buy, which of your friends to invite, and so forth. Your approach to social situations and activities will probably differ as well. Your 6 suggests you will be more extroverted than usual, reaching out to others, while your partner seeks quiet time alone.

Positive influences during this cycle are found in your tolerance, generosity, and willingness to sacrifice to accommodate your partner. This is an important and necessary factor for the relationship during this time.

Your partner may not be as patient as usual and may seem withdrawn. But if your partner seems a bit cool and distant, it probably has nothing to do with the relationship; your partner is just doing a little soul-searching and needs space. However, they should also be cautious about becoming so focused on their own world that they lose sight of you. Although your partner's 7 inspires a more inward, personal journey, they need to recognize that loved ones need attention too.

Your partner's monthly number is 8

Although they are quite different, your cycles are very compatible. You both should experience progress in your career and other practical, material endeavors. This is a favorable cycle with the potential to bring progress and possibly a financial windfall.

On a personal level, you will probably be more involved with each other as well, albeit in very different ways. Your 6 will be focused on matters of the heart, so you should feel strongly committed and eager to make your partner happy. Your cycle will focus on home, family, friends, and practical issues.

Your partner's 8 will awaken leadership skills and ambition—even within the relationship. This could pose problems, because your partner's tact and sensitivity may not be as keen as usual. Your partner is taking more control over their life, which is an integral part of this cycle, but they must be careful not to carry that attitude into the relationship. You need love, not leadership.

Your partner should focus their ambition on goals, and their heart on the relationship.

Your partner's monthly number is 9

Although this may be an emotional period for your partner, it is considered a very compatible cycle combination.

Your 6 should help you feel especially devoted and committed to the relationship during this period, which is exactly what your partner needs. Your partner could feel a little worn out and rudderless or have concerns that expectations have not been met. Mood swings and doubt can cause havoc during a 9 cycle, when loose ends need to be tied up.

You, on the other hand, should feel stable and be able to offer comfort and support. Your 6 inspires love, nurturing, and concern for others. This is also a favorable time for you to focus on practical matters, especially those relating to home, family, and career.

Much will depend on your ability to offer encouragement and reassurance; and your partner offers important insight as well, bringing moments of clarity and an enhanced perspective to your mutual goals and expectations. Your partner brings inspiration born of an urgency to figure out what is happening and where to go next. Like adrenaline for the soul, moments of apprehension or fear can help them see more clearly.

Love, commitment, and sacrifice are the main ingredients in both of your cycles. However, because your 6 lends an especially warm, personal connection, you should be able to help lessen the emotional tenderness that is likely to accompany your partner's transitional cycle.

CHAPTER 7

Month Cycle 7

Your partner's monthly number is 1

During these cycles, the challenge for a relationship is to maintain a feeling of belonging. While there are significant differences in how the 7 and 1 cycles affect us, they both increase our awareness of independence and individuality. It is natural to experience some distance in your relationship during this period, and it is not necessarily a negative thing.

If your expectation is to spend a great deal of time together, sharing everything, and resisting any change, you may find your experience falling short. It is wise to accept that you will likely grow somewhat apart during this period as a temporary and necessary part of personal growth, ultimately contributing to the stability and harmony of your relationship.

Your partner is experiencing a 1 cycle, indicating their focus on career or other personal goals, actively seizing opportunities for progress. Meanwhile, your attention is turned inward, toward spiritual and mental growth. You are undergoing a period of self-discovery and require time alone as a vital part of this transformative process.

Although your needs differ in nature, both of you require a period of self-focus rather than focusing solely on each other. This may create a perception that the relationship is weakening. However, unless you turn it into an issue, this does not have to be the case. By accepting the fact that both of you are currently focused elsewhere, you will discover that this period offers personal growth without jeopardizing the foundation of your relationship.

Your partner's monthly number is 2

During this period, your individual cycles diverge significantly, but they shouldn't pose many challenges to your relationship.

Your partner may experience heightened sensitivity. However, it's important for them not to overly attach significance to their emotional ups and downs. This period is best suited for them to focus on practical matters and determine their priorities.

At times, it may feel like you are distant and residing in a world that excludes your partner. In a sense, this is true. You are going through a phase of self-reflection, delving into the inner mysteries of life from philosophical, intellectual, or spiritual perspectives. As for your partner, their optimal response is to concentrate on their own life, particularly the practical aspects of their career, home, finances, and other relevant areas.

If either of you perceives that the other is prioritizing their individual needs over the relationship, it's crucial to understand that this is not necessarily negative, selfish, or indicative of trouble in the relationship. Your needs and priorities are simply different at the moment. Rest assured, the relationship remains secure as neither of you desires to disrupt the stability. Allowing each other the space and freedom to pursue individual interests can ultimately strengthen your bond.

Your partner's monthly number is 3

The combination of the 7 and 3 cycles brings together two distinctly contrasting influences. Your numbers embody opposite energies and influences.

For your partner, this period promises a lightening of spirits, akin to the emergence of the sun after a series of overcast days. For you, your 7 cycle signifies a time of introspection, self-awareness, and personal exploration. It is a period of quietude and inward focus for you, while your partner experiences the exact opposite. They are likely to be more sociable, playful, and even a bit scattered, devoid of a tranquil disposition.

The stark contrast in moods can potentially hinder effective communication and lead to frustration. Your partner's cheerful and carefree demeanor may struggle to relate to your contemplative and possibly pessimistic outlook. Conversely, you may find it challenging to connect with their sunny and optimistic state of mind.

To address this challenge, it is crucial to acknowledge and respond to each other's concerns. Express your love and affection, extend a helping hand, and grant each other the space to pursue individual interests.

It is important for your partner to recognize that your current introspective phase is temporary yet necessary. By the same token, you should strive to avoid irritation with their seemingly superficial attitude, which may not align with your introspective nature.

This combination of cycles can potentially strain relationships. If you sense that you are approaching precarious territory, it is essential to communicate your feelings promptly and honestly. Although both of you will be affected by your individual cycles, the impact may be more pronounced on your end.

Supporting each other to the best of your abilities during this period is paramount. Remember, cycles are inherently transient. Patience and tolerance serve as guiding principles for both of you as you navigate this phase together.

Your partner's monthly number is 4

This combination of cycles has the potential to create a sense of distance between you, not because your interest in each other diminishes but because your individual cycles generate divergent interests and concerns that pull you in separate directions.

For your partner, this is a period characterized by attending to practical and mundane matters, which they may perceive as tedious and frustrating. On the other hand, your cycle's emphasis on the number 7 draws your focus inward, inviting moments of introspection, daydreaming, grappling with doubts and questions, and deepening your understanding of your true self. It becomes evident how these contrasting needs intrinsic to your cycles can contribute to a sense of distance.

To alleviate strain in your relationship and seize the opportunities for growth offered by this cycle, it is crucial to share your feelings openly and to provide each other with the space to pursue individual interests. By doing so, you can navigate the challenges posed by your differing cycles while making progress in your personal journeys.

Your partner's monthly number is 5

In the current phase of your journey together, both you and your partner find yourselves deeply immersed in one of the most transformative and affectionate cycles, despite the striking numerical contrast between 7 and 5. What's truly remarkable is how seamlessly you harmonize despite these disparities.

Your partner is going through a phase marked by dynamic change and vibrant energy. They're in a state of flux, eagerly embracing new experiences and opportunities. In contrast, you might notice yourself gravitating toward introspection and withdrawal. This is a time when you're engrossed in self-discovery, charting your own unique path forward.

While your individual cycles exert distinct influences on each of you—your partner radiating outward, and you being drawn inward—the beauty lies in how these differences complement one another through mutual support. Your contemplative, inward-focused energy can be intriguing to your partner, especially during moments when they crave subtle, mysterious experiences that spark their curiosity. Conversely, their energetic enthusiasm and inspiring demeanor can have a positive influence on you, providing a welcome connection to the external world when you may be yearning for it.

However, it's crucial to recognize that your partner might misinterpret your subdued attitude as a sign that something is amiss. It's essential for them to refrain from jumping to such a conclusion. During a 7 cycle, the last thing one desires is to be pulled away from their introspective space, and you might find any attempts at intrusion to be bothersome.

The key to navigating this phase harmoniously is to embrace your inherent disparities and allow yourselves to simply coexist. By doing so, you create an opportunity for intimacy and mutual appreciation. This unique blend of energies can lead to a connection where both of you have the chance to grow and thrive in your own ways, while simultaneously nurturing the bond that makes your partnership so special.

Your partner's monthly number is 6

You and your partner currently find yourselves navigating vastly different territories. The intricate interplay of the energies represented by the numbers 7 and 6 creates a fascinating and complementary dynamic. However, it's important to acknowledge that these divergent needs may leave you with limited common ground during this period.

As you traverse this phase, it's quite possible that disagreements will surface in various aspects of your lives. You may find yourselves at odds over decisions like how to spend your leisure time, which car to purchase, or even which friends to invite into your circle. Your approaches to social situations and activities may also diverge significantly. Your partner may exhibit a more extroverted nature during this time, reaching out to connect with others and actively engaging in social interactions. In contrast, you are inclined toward solitary moments and introspection.

Nevertheless, amid the potential challenges, there are positive elements that come to light within this cycle. Your partner's tolerance, generous spirit, and willingness to make sacrifices to accommodate you play pivotal roles in your relationship during this period. Your partner's capacity to understand and adapt to your introspective nature can be a source of strength and harmony, even when the external circumstances may seem at odds.

On the flip side, you might notice yourself being less patient than usual. If you find yourself seeming cool or distant at times, it's important to recognize that it's likely not a reflection of your feelings for the relationship. Instead, it stems from your need for introspection and personal space. Therefore, it's crucial to remain mindful of your partner's needs and avoid becoming overly absorbed in your own world. While the influence of the number 7 may inspire an inward, personal journey, your loved ones, including your partner, still require your attention, care, and presence in their lives.

By respecting each other's individual needs and inclinations, you can navigate these differences with grace and understanding, ultimately strengthening your bond, and learning valuable lessons that will contribute to the growth and resilience of your relationship.

Your partner's monthly number is 7

This is a period when you should have a great deal of control over the way you experience your relationship. In most societies, the 7 cycle can be the most difficult to live up to—not because it is demanding but because it asks you to back away from the daily grind. It is a time to give to yourself and your deeper spiritual and intellectual needs. The inner journey is not encouraged by most cultures; yet, without periods of self-examination, we can get lost in the day-to-day routine and forget to slow down and appreciate life's nonmaterial pleasures and mysteries.

The way you choose to approach this cycle will be the deciding factor in how it affects you and your relationship. If you have learned how to coexist quietly without constantly demanding each other's attention, you will have a big advantage, for that is precisely what this cycle asks from you. You are both experiencing a time when you need to be alone more than usual. You may find that you have little patience for those you perceive as intrusive, and this does not exclude your partner.

Do your best to stay connected, but try to support each other's need for solitude and individual pursuits. Taking time to learn more about yourself can be of benefit to your relationship as well.

Your partner's monthly number is 8

This cycle will produce very different influences and needs for each of you. You may feel a little left out or ignored by your partner, although this is most likely not their intention. Your partner's cycle is just focused on getting things done, reaching goals, and taking advantage of opportunities, at a time when you are more contemplative, examining your priorities, and perhaps questioning the reasons behind what you are doing.

The fact that you and your partner's needs and ambitions are moving in different directions could create problems for your relationship. You may find it difficult to find common ground or even be interested in each other's concerns.

Your best approach during this cycle is to give each other room to pursue your differing interests and to avoid feeling you must share everything. You will need more time alone than usual, to reflect and analyze, or just to enjoy a little solitude. During this cycle, it is probably best to keep things simple and allow for a little separation in your daily lives.

Your partner's monthly number is 9

You may feel somewhat distant from each other during this cycle, as you are both likely to feel emotions that are not easily articulated or understood. Although you share the need to be more inwardly focused than usual, your experiences will probably be quite dissimilar.

You are seeking clarity, understanding, increased self-awareness, and growth (although this may be somewhat subconscious). Your partner also has an inward focus, but on a more practical and emotional level. The 9 could make them feel less confident than usual, so doubts and questions are likely to arise.

Although you will also share this questioning state of mind, you should feel stronger and more capable than your partner, who will probably feel more vulnerable than normal. You can be a much-needed source of strength for your partner during this period. Your partner doesn't necessarily expect answers from you, but they could use your emotional support. However, although your partner will probably need the closeness you can provide, they should respect that you will also need more time alone than usual.

This is a learning cycle for both of you, with the potential to leave you stronger spiritually and emotionally.

CHAPTER 8

Month Cycle 8

Your partner's monthly number is 1

On the surface, the combination of 1 and 8 appears excellent, but it conceals some potential pitfalls. The upside is that it will ignite a sense of drive and progress in both of you, propelling you toward your respective goals, albeit in different ways. Your partner possesses a clear direction, while you may struggle with decisiveness and face some uncertainty despite your considerable efforts.

Both of you are traversing paths of progress, although your partner's journey is straightforward, while your goals are less defined but potentially rewarding. By the end of this cycle, you may stumble upon a promising investment opportunity or experience a financial windfall, opening new possibilities.

However, it is important to acknowledge the substantial gap between these cycles, stemming from your different spiritual paths. This distinction may become more apparent during this period and could create some stress within the relationship. Although much of it may be inconsequential, it is advisable to ignore insignificant issues. While maintaining a healthy relationship often requires open discussions about differences, there are occasions when it is better to avoid touchy subjects and embrace the fact that you are individuals with varying opinions and approaches. This is a time to set aside those differences and simply revel in each other's company.

Both of you are currently experiencing cycles that enhance your material position. Therefore, your best approach during this period is to focus on that aspect. As for any contrasts in intellectual or spiritual viewpoints, it would be wiser to address them at another time.

Your partner's monthly number is 2

This combination of cycles presents a significant challenge due to misaligned priorities. Your partner places great importance on the relationship and matters of the heart, leading to heightened sensitivity and emotions. During this period, they may become more susceptible to criticism or perceived neglect.

Meanwhile, your focus shifts toward other areas of life. Career, finances, friends, and family take precedence for you. Your intention is to enhance everything that surrounds and supports the relationship. However, this shift in focus may lead to a lack of attention from your partner's perspective. They might feel that you aren't shouldering enough emotional weight, when, in reality, your focus is simply directed elsewhere.

The combination of these cycles creates opportunities for misunderstandings and disagreements. It is likely that you will encounter rough patches, but there are also positive aspects to be found. You have the potential to make improvements in areas outside the relationship, which ultimately contribute to its overall support and well-being. Simultaneously, your partner can play a crucial role in maintaining your connection and deepening the bond between you both.

Your partner's monthly number is 3

Your cycles, although distinct, harmonize remarkably well. Your partner's cycle is infused with creativity, optimism, and inspiration, while yours revolves around ambition, goals, and financial rewards. These divergent influences complement and uplift one another, fostering a positive impact on your relationship as well as practical, everyday affairs.

Now is an opportune moment to tend to long-delayed projects, such as financial matters, home repairs, and other practical concerns. Furthermore, this combination bodes exceptionally well for relationships. You will find that you relate and communicate effortlessly, readily supporting each other's endeavors.

However, there exists a potential source of discord. Your partner's 3 cycle imbues them with inspiration and liveliness but also renders them less focused and disciplined than usual. Meanwhile, you are fully engrossed in a period of heightened concentration, particularly concerning the bottom line. Consequently, you may perceive your partner as somewhat irresponsible, while they might perceive you as all work and no play.

To navigate this potential challenge, it is crucial to embrace compromise and acknowledge the distinct aspects of your respective cycles. Doing so will enable a deeper understanding of your partner's perspective and allow both of you to capitalize on the abundant opportunities presented during this period.

Your partner's monthly number is 4

This cycle's combination can yield either highly positive or rather negative outcomes, leaving little room for a middle ground.

For your partner, this period represents slow progress and considerable frustration, and it demands substantial effort. Conversely, you will likely find that everything falls into place effortlessly, as if there for the taking.

Within your relationship, this combination has the power to bring out the best in both of you, or it might amplify negative tendencies. Your optimistic and ambitious attitude can either prove bothersome to your partner or serve as a source of comfort, easing their frustration and anxiety. Similarly, their dedicated and methodical approach can either inspire and motivate you or dampen your dynamic energy.

To complicate matters further, you will likely have heightened awareness of the impact you have on each other during this period. Consequently, your interactions can evoke feelings of love, appreciation, irritation, or blame, depending on how you choose to respond to each other.

The key to maximizing the benefits of this cycle lies in cultivating sensitivity toward your partner's needs and state of mind. Strive to avoid becoming so absorbed in your own world that you lose touch with theirs; foster open communication and empathy to maintain a harmonious balance.

Your partner's monthly number is 5

In this whirlwind of a cycle, it feels like challenges are converging upon you and your partner simultaneously, creating a landscape in which keeping up with the relentless pace of life can be quite demanding. Your partner finds themselves navigating a delicate balancing act, juggling an array of responsibilities, and shouldering a more extensive load of tasks than usual. In contrast, your visionary outlook and unwavering ambition have you locked onto your plans and the many opportunities that beckon you forward.

The stark disparities in the energies influencing each of you during this period might, at times, leave little room to simply relish each other's presence. Nevertheless, there's no cause for alarm, because a more tranquil phase awaits in your next cycle. During that period, both of you will pivot your focus toward nurturing your relationship and cherishing quality moments with family and friends.

Within your partner's cycle, change is key, although it may take several cycles for the full scope of these transformations to become apparent. Picture their energy as a multitude of atoms in constant motion, bouncing in myriad directions as they explore new territories and set boundaries in various aspects of life. On the flip side, your cycle stands in stark contrast as a beacon of intense focus, enabling you to zero in on your next objective with laser-like precision, centered on a single focal point.

One of the most common pitfalls that couples face in this particular blend of energies is the temptation to impose their own perspective on each other. Such attempts can lead to frustration and stymie the potential for growth within this cycle. Instead, it is absolutely vital to afford each other the freedom to pursue individual goals without the weighty baggage of excessive explanations or the need to justify one's actions. By nurturing this sense of autonomy, you'll foster an environment where both of your unique energies can flourish, ultimately paving the way for a stronger, more harmonious connection between the two of you.

Your partner's monthly number is 6

What stands out with this combination of cycles is their compatibility, despite their differences. Both of you find yourselves at a juncture where progress in your careers and practical, material pursuits are not only attainable but highly promising. This favorable cycle holds the potential for advancement and perhaps the possibility of a financial windfall.

On a personal level, your connection is poised to deepen, through distinct and meaningful avenues. For your partner, the 6 cycle will revolve around matters of the heart, fostering a sense of commitment and a desire to bring you happiness. Their focus will gravitate toward the nurturing realms of home, family, friends, and practical considerations that sustain and enrich your shared life.

Conversely, your 8 cycle signals the awakening of your leadership abilities and a surge of ambition, even within the context of your relationship. However, it's important to recognize that this newfound assertiveness may pose certain challenges, as your usual tact and sensitivity may not be as finely honed during this phase. While taking charge of your own life aligns with the essence of this cycle, it's equally crucial to exercise caution and avoid carrying this dominant attitude into the relationship. What your partner truly needs during this time is your love and support, not your leadership.

So, the key is to direct your ambition toward personal goals and pursuits while keeping your heart devoted to nurturing the relationship. Striking a balance between your personal ambitions and your role as a partner will be vital. In doing so, you can make the most of this cycle, seizing career opportunities and achieving personal milestones while ensuring that your relationship thrives with the warmth, love, and understanding that your partner values most.

Your partner's monthly number is 7

Within the current cycle, you'll find divergent influences and needs unfolding for you and your partner. It's essential to acknowledge these differences to ensure an amicable journey through this phase.

Your primary focus during this time is centered on accomplishment, the pursuit of your goals, and a keen readiness to seize every opportunity that comes your way. Your ambitions drive you forward with fervor and determination. Meanwhile, your partner's mindset tends to lean more toward introspection—a period of evaluating their priorities, questioning the motivations behind their actions, and delving into the depths of their thoughts.

The disparity between your respective needs and ambitions has the potential to create challenges within your relationship. Finding common ground may indeed prove challenging, and there's a possibility that mutual interest in each other's concerns could wane, driven by the strong pull of your individual journeys. When that is the case, remember that it's just a cycle and will pass soon enough.

It's crucial to grant each other space and freedom without feeling the need to share every aspect of your experiences. Your partner may find that they require more solitude than usual, whether for deep reflection, introspective analysis, or simply to savor moments of solitude that nurture their inner world.

Embracing simplicity and maintaining a certain level of separation in your daily lives might be the most suitable approach during this period and can provide the necessary breathing room for both of you to honor your unique paths and fulfill your individual needs.

Your partner's monthly number is 8

You share the same cycle number. Since cycles follow each other in a repeating sequence, you will always share the same personal cycle numbers, and consequently the same influences.

Your 8 can bring the best or the worst of times—usually a bit of both. With help and effort, you can tip the balance favorably, but you should be prepared to experience challenges as well.

On the positive side, it should be a period of ambition and reward for both of you. This cycle brings strength, focus, the potential for progress, and possibly rewards from past efforts. In addition, you should find it easier than usual to support and strengthen those qualities in each other.

On the negative side, it might also intensify your less desirable qualities. You could find you're both a bit more self-centered than usual, perhaps even ruthless in the pursuit of your goals. It is likely you will be focused on yourself and less interested in giving than in receiving.

If you both aim your energies at the external world, everything should be fine. However, should you find your partner in the crosshairs, remember what is most important to you and be careful to prioritize your relationship. This cycle and its influences will move on—don't let its competitive tone get the better of your relationship.

Your partner's monthly number is 9

As is often the case in your relationship, this cycle influences you in very different and not altogether compatible ways.

For you, it is a time to get out and shake some trees, make things happen, and reap the rewards. To make the most of this cycle, it will be important for you to stay focused and aggressive while pursuing your goals.

For your partner, the cycle could feel a little shaky, so they will need your commitment and support during this period. With your focus on interests outside the relationship, and your partner needing your attention more than usual, it will probably take effort from both of you to prevent disappointment or resentment from creeping in.

Although this will be an enterprising time for you, make time for your partner as well. You too will experience a period when nothing seems secure and solid. In fact, your next cycle will probably bring a bit of that, so you may be looking to them for support.

Help your partner recognize you do not mean to pull away from them, your cycle just delivers a more ambitious spirit. Your partner is at the end of a cycle and should focus on completing projects and letting go of things that are no longer fruitful. (Your partner's next cycle should be much more energetic.)

Because your cycles tend to be almost opposite, you have probably learned to adjust to each other's needs. This ability is the key to sustaining a long and happy union.

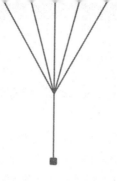

CHAPTER 9

Month Cycle 9

Your partner's monthly number is 1

Your relationship is currently entering a challenging period, occurring once every nine cycles, where your love and commitment will be tested. This phase is likely to bring about disagreements and arguments that may leave you questioning the transformation of the person you once knew. The root cause lies in the fact that you and your partner find yourselves at opposite ends of the spectrum. Your partner is currently in a 1 cycle, brimming with energy, optimism, new ideas, and plans. On the other hand, you find yourself at the tail end of your cycles, which brings a sense of completion, finality, and a general feeling of fatigue, stress, and decreased motivation across the board. Conflicts can escalate rapidly, particularly because of your emotional vulnerability during this period, while your partner may be less sensitive than usual.

This combination of cycles presents one of the most challenging dynamics, but with dedicated effort and recognition of your love for each other, your relationship can not only survive but also grow stronger. For your partner, the most crucial piece of advice is to shower you with ample attention; they should be mindful of your potential mood swings, even if they perceive you as overly dramatic—a sentiment that might hold some truth.

As for you, it is essential not to take your emotions too seriously. The changes you are going through require surrender and acceptance. It will also be beneficial to realize that they do not intend to be abrupt or insensitive; rather, your partner is simply operating within a more energetic and upbeat cycle than you.

Ultimately, it is your hearts that hold the key to salvation. In times of heightened emotions, it is often the heart, rather than the mind, that can truly understand and endure the storm.

Your partner's monthly number is 2

During this cycle, you will have the opportunity to assess the foundation of your relationship. While your experiences may vary, your numbers indicate that both of you are entering a period where emotions take center stage.

Your partner will exhibit a somewhat self-absorbed and emotional demeanor, seemingly in response to everything around them. They will be more vulnerable and sensitive, developing a heightened intuition to discern what is genuine from what is not. To gain clarity, they need to shed protective layers, which might leave them feeling exposed and vulnerable.

On the other hand, your 9 cycle brings about a distinct, yet equally emotionally charged period. Your focus is less on the relationship itself and more on making important choices as you approach a crossroads in your life. This cycle holds great significance for you, as it encompasses growth, completion, and decision-making, but it is also likely to be filled with emotional ups and downs.

As you navigate through your individual journeys during this cycle, your ability to support each other may be limited to offering reassurance of your love. By weathering this time together, you will gain valuable insight into the resilience of your relationship when faced with divergent needs and goals.

If your relationship is built on a solid foundation, you will emerge from this period with strength and harmony. Even if challenges arise, they will provide valuable lessons about how your relationship can endure in times of differing individual needs and objectives.

Your partner's monthly number is 3

This combination of cycles is wonderfully compatible and holds the potential for birthing new ideas and plans. It is a time that will ignite enhanced creativity in both of you, opening doors to change and improvement.

However, amidst this period of excitement, you may encounter a challenging phase of intense emotions that calls for a stable environment and unwavering support from your partner. Fortunately, their cycle radiates optimism and positivity, serving as a much-needed source of comfort for you.

Given the inevitable differences in your approaches and attitudes, it is crucial to honor and respect each other's needs during this cycle. Your partner can play a vital role by exercising patience and understanding if you find yourself less grounded than usual. You may be navigating a time of profound choices and decisions, even on a subconscious level, which can render things unclear and complex for you.

On the other hand, your partner should embrace an upbeat, carefree approach to life during this cycle, enjoying a relatively smoother and less emotionally charged time. While there may be ups and downs, their challenge lies in maintaining direction and focus.

Although it may not appear to be the ideal time for significant changes, the process of jointly making plans can contribute to a greater sense of security for both of you.

Throughout this period, your partner's ability to be a pillar of strength and a source of comfort will play a pivotal role. Your 9 cycle is considered the most demanding, while theirs tends to be one of ease and enjoyment. This fortuitous combination allows them to share their positive energy with you during your more challenging phase, nurturing the relationship and fostering mutual growth.

Your partner's monthly number is 4

The combination of the 9 and the 4 cycles often breeds emotional turbulence within a relationship.

In your case, being at the end of a cycle leaves you feeling somewhat weary, leading to unpredictable emotional states. You are urged to release the past and ready yourself for new beginnings, inevitably stirring intense sentiments. Conversely, your partner's 4 cycle fixates on practical matters, leaving little space for empathy. Their focus centers on career, projects, details, diligence, discipline, and tangible progress.

During this time, you require understanding and a shared sense of purpose. Your partner may yearn for you to concentrate more on immediate practicalities and tasks at hand.

Recognizing that you both navigate distinct stages is crucial. To nurture your relationship during this cycle, maintaining closeness is paramount. Dedicate effort to focus more on your partner and less on yourself, breaking away from mundane routines to engage in activities you both find joy in.

Your partner's monthly number is 5

This combination of cycles ushers in a period of considerable challenges. Many of the doubts and questions that arise during this time may go unanswered, casting a sense of ambiguity over your journey. As the curtain falls on your 9 cycle, you may find yourself grappling with feelings of weariness and vulnerability. However, you can take comfort in the fact that your next cycle brings renewed energy—a phase that promises to be uplifting, inspiring, and deeply empowering.

Your partner, on the other hand, is likely to experience a surge of energy, albeit with a hint of reduced patience compared to their usual self. Their 5 cycle brings with it a dynamic drive and the potential for a few changes in the landscape of your shared life. Their innate ability to infuse excitement and enthusiasm into the relationship can serve as a wonderful elixir, invigorating your connection and adding zest to your shared experiences.

It's worth noting that both the 9 and 5 cycles revolve around the concept of change, albeit manifesting in contrasting ways. The changes brought about by the 5 cycle are driven by excitement, enthusiasm, and an innate desire to shake things up, injecting a dose of adventure into your lives. On the other hand, your 9 cycle centers on personal growth, often leading to phases of completion and purification, which can be emotionally challenging as they navigate the depths of self-discovery.

In this period, patience emerges as the most crucial ingredient in maximizing the benefits of these divergent cycles. Your partner will require your patience during moments of uncertainty, and you, in turn, must gather your strength to offer unwavering support.

By weathering this challenging phase with understanding and fortitude, both of you pave the way for a more harmonious future, enriched by the diversity of your experiences.

Your partner's monthly number is 6

In this emotionally charged cycle combination, you and your partner discover an unexpected yet remarkable compatibility.

During this period, your partner's 6 cycle sets the stage for a transformation in your relationship. Their devotion and commitment to the partnership align completely with what you require. On the other hand, you might find yourself in a state of emotional flux, occasionally experiencing fatigue and moments of uncertainty, as the 9 cycle typically makes one feel somewhat worn out. Mood swings and doubts can make their presence felt, which can be challenging for your partner. Fortunately, it's precisely during these moments that your partner shines. Their 6 cycle offers a steady and stable anchor, characterized by love, nurturing, and a genuine concern for others. This is also an opportune time for them to focus on practical matters, particularly those related to the home, family, and career. Their innate ability to provide encouragement and reassurance plays a pivotal role in supporting you during this, for you have a somewhat difficult transformative phase.

As you navigate this cycle together, you'll find that your partner's warmth and intimacy enhance the emotional stability of your relationship. You, in turn, bring invaluable insight, infusing moments of clarity and an enriched perspective into your shared aspirations and expectations.

Both of your cycles embrace love, commitment, and the willingness to make sacrifices as fundamental ingredients. With your partner's 6 cycle fostering a warm and intimate connection, they have the power to alleviate the emotional sensitivity that often accompanies your 9 cycle. Together, you form a strong and balanced partnership, where each of you contributes unique strengths to complement the other, making this period of emotional transformation a deeply enriching and mutually rewarding experience.

Your partner's monthly number is 7

Within this cycle, it's not uncommon to sense a subtle emotional distance between you and your partner, as both of you are likely to grapple with emotions that are intricate and at times challenging to put into words or to fully comprehend.

For your partner, the primary focus is on a quest for clarity, understanding, and personal growth, even if these inner transformations occur at a subconscious level. This journey is deeply personal and meaningful to them. On the other hand, your inward focus tends to be more grounded in practical and emotional aspects. The influence of the 9 cycle may bring with it a temporary lack of confidence, causing doubts and questions to surface as you navigate this phase.

While the two of you share this contemplative state of mind, it's worth noting that your partner may exhibit greater strength and resilience compared to you during this time, as you might find yourself feeling more vulnerable than usual. In this regard, your partner can serve as a vital source of support. The emotional reassurance they offer can prove invaluable as you navigate the intricate labyrinth of your emotions. However, it's equally crucial to recognize and respect their need for increased solitude during this period, even though your natural inclination may be toward seeking closeness and connection.

This cycle serves as a profound learning experience for both you and your partner. It has the potential to cultivate not only spiritual and emotional fortitude but also a deeper understanding of yourselves and each other. Despite the temporary emotional distance that may arise, this journey can ultimately leave both of you stronger, more resilient, and with a more profound appreciation for the complexities of the human experience within the context of your relationship.

Your partner's monthly number is 8

For your partner, this period is a time to venture out boldly, to make daring moves, and to reap the well-deserved rewards of current and previous efforts. To fully harness the potential of this cycle, it's imperative for your partner to maintain unwavering focus, assertiveness, and an unrelenting pursuit of their goals.

Conversely, you may find yourself grappling with a sense of uncertainty during this phase, which magnifies the importance of your partner's commitment and support. As they divert their attention toward interests beyond the boundaries of your relationship, and you, in turn, seek their presence more ardently than usual, both of you must make a conscious effort to prevent disappointment and resentment from creeping into your shared space.

Amid your partner's enterprising pursuits, it's equally vital for them to reserve time and energy for you. The pursuit of their ambitions may lead them into a phase where stability feels elusive and uncertain, possibly in their upcoming cycle. During such moments, they may naturally turn to you for support, as you've been a steady anchor in their life.

Communication is paramount here. Your partner must convey that their focus on their own ambitions doesn't imply a desire to distance themselves from you. Rather, it signifies a period where their ambitious spirit takes center stage. Meanwhile, you find yourself approaching the culmination of your cycle, a time when it's advisable to wrap up ongoing projects and let go of endeavors that no longer bear fruit. No worries; the promise of a more dynamic and energetic upcoming cycle lies on the horizon.

Given the near-opposite nature of your cycles, it's evident that you both have learned the art of adaptability, accommodating each other's needs with grace and understanding. This adaptability is a cornerstone in nurturing a lasting and fulfilling union, one that continues to evolve and thrive even amid the ebbs and flows of your individual cycles.

Your partner's monthly number is 9

This is likely to be a challenging period for both of you. However, although some cycles will be favorable, and others less so, you will almost always relate to each other more easily than most couples because you share the same cycles, so you understand how your partner feels.

The challenging aspect of this cycle lies in your shared need for each other's support at a time when neither of you is as capable of giving as you might like. You both seek stability, which might feel in short supply right now. You both feel uninspired and low on energy, which could leave you with less to give. Fortunately, this period is not made of shadows alone; it also has a bright side. The 9 can help you recognize more clearly what you want from life. Think of it as a cross-country trip where you need to stop occasionally to study the map and plan the next part of your journey. It can help keep you on track and add clarity and focus.

Do your best to stay connected and support each other as you end this cycle together. Fortunately, your next cycle brings fresh new energy.

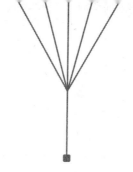

Conclusion

Numerology offers profound insights into the dynamics of love and relationships, revealing the hidden patterns and energies that influence our connections with others. As we have explored throughout this book, numbers are more than mere symbols; they are potent forces that shape and reflect our personalities, behaviors, and interactions. By understanding the numerical essence of ourselves and our partners, we can unlock the potential for harmony and minimize discord within our relationships, paving the way for deeper connection and mutual understanding.

In this book, we focused on the Life Path number, which represents our fundamental life journey and purpose, playing a crucial role in compatibility. However, we are not confined by the influence of our Life Path numbers. On the contrary, we possess the power to change and reshape ourselves, and that is an awesome power. While you have likely learned a lot about your own number and that of your partner, I encourage you to read about the other numbers as well—to learn about the other people in your lives, as well as other aspects of yourself.

Ultimately, the journey of love and relationships is one of continual growth and discovery. Numerology can serve as a guide, illuminating the paths that lead to deeper connections and understanding. It reminds us that every relationship, regardless of its numerical composition, holds the potential for profound learning and transformation.

As we conclude this exploration of numerology in love and relationships, let us embrace the wisdom that numbers offer. By integrating this knowledge into our lives, we can cultivate relationships that are harmonious, enriching, and empowering. Whether you are just beginning a new relationship or seeking to deepen an existing one, may the insights of numerology guide you toward greater love, understanding, and fulfillment.

Numbers are the hidden choreographers in the dance of life, guiding our steps and shaping our interactions. By attuning ourselves to their rhythms, we can move with greater grace and harmony, creating relationships that are not only numerically compatible but also deeply connected on a soulful level. Let us continue to explore and honor the wisdom of numbers, allowing their insights to illuminate our path toward love and unity.

May your journey in numerology and relationships be filled with discovery, joy, and fulfillment.

ACKNOWLEDGMENTS

I owe a heartfelt thank-you to Julie Hall, whose love and encouragement helped me through some challenging times. To Janice Tirapelli, my business partner (and occasional therapist), for tolerating my grumpiness. And to Lauren Appleton, my editor, for her incredible patience and support. Without them, this book might still be gathering metaphorical dust on my hard drive.

I also want to express my deep gratitude to the many numerologists whose works I studied: Kevin Q. Avery, Cheiro (William John Warner), Juno Jordan, Lloyd Strayhorn, Matthew Goodwin, Julia Seton, Faith Javane, Thomas Muldoon, Ruth Drayer, Lynn Buess, Linda Goodman, Dusty Bunker, Dr. Carl Jung, and Robert Thomas Cross, to name a few.